Jane Pettigrew's
TEA TIME

Jane Pettigrew's
TEA TIME

A COMPLETE COLLECTION
OF TRADITIONAL
RECIPES

DORLING KINDERSLEY ◆ LONDON

Editor Joanna Lorenz
Designer Hugh Schermuly
Art Director Peter Luff

Photography by James Murphy
Cover and inside illustrations by Antonia Enthoven

First published in Great Britain in 1986 by
Dorling Kindersley Publishers Limited,
9 Henrietta Street, London WC2E 8PS

First published as a Dorling Kindersley paperback 1988
Reprinted 1989, 1990, 1991, 1992, 1994

British Library Cataloguing in Publication Data
Pettigrew, Jane
  Tea-time.
  1. Afternoon teas
  I. Title
  641.5′3   TX736

ISBN 0-86318-297-6

Printed in Hong Kong by Wing King Tong Co. Ltd

CONTENTS

PREFACE

At 4 o'clock in the afternoon there is nothing quite so refreshing and revitalizing as a cup of tea, and I feel that taking tea in the afternoon should be more than just brewing a quick cup from a tea-bag. If time allows, it should be a restful, social occasion with the refinements of a pretty table-cloth, napkins, fine china and a vase of flowers on the table.

When the Tea-Time tea-shop was opened in August 1983, we tried to recreate the atmosphere and style of the tea-shops which thrived in England in the 1930s and 1940s. We wanted people to feel comfortable and relaxed, to enjoy a peaceful cup of tea with a home-made sandwich or cake while listening to the music of the big dance bands, palm court trios and film songs of the period. The visitors to Tea-Time do seem to enjoy the nostalgic flavour, and sometimes comment on how nice it is to 'do things properly'!

The range of teas on offer at Tea-Time has recently been increased, to reflect the growing interest in different varieties of tea. In widening my own experience and enjoyment of tea I have been given invaluable help and information by Sam Twining, of the well known tea company of the same name. I would like to thank him for his enthusiastic interest in this book and his willingness to share his own love and knowledge of tea and tea drinking with me.

THE ENGLISH ART OF AFTERNOON TEA

The English custom of taking afternoon tea is thought to have been started in the nineteenth century by Anna, the Seventh Duchess of Bedford. Luncheon in those days was rather early and dinner was not served until 8 or 9 o'clock in the evening. Every afternoon the Duchess found that she was rather hungry and started taking a pot of tea with some light refreshments in her room each day between 3 and 4 o'clock. She began inviting friends to join her, and soon taking tea in the middle of the afternoon became the fashionable thing to do. Elegant tea-ware also became available, making afternoon tea even more of a special occasion: lace and embroidered table linen, tea services in silver or gold or fine bone china, creamers, teaspoons, tea knives, cake stands, cake servers, sandwich trays, tea caddies containing tea canisters and blending bowls, sugar tongs and pretty tea strainers.

Today, as in the Duchess of Bedford's time, it is usual for the host or hostess to pour the tea and to hand round the sandwiches and cakes. Guests are seated either around a ready-laid table or in armchairs with side tables for the cups, saucers and plates. Each guest should have a cup and saucer, a teaspoon, a side plate, a napkin, a tea knife for spreading butter and preserves and a pastry fork if cakes are to be served. In the centre of the table is the teapot, a jug of hot water to refill the teapot, a slop bowl for discarded tea leaves, a tea strainer, a milk jug or creamer and a sugar bowl. If lump or cube sugar is offered, sugar tongs should be provided, and also slices of lemon and lemon squeezers for those guests who do not take milk in their tea.

The choice of food and type of tea served can vary according to taste and time of year. A summer tea held in the open air usually includes a selection of sandwiches, scones, jams and clotted cream, pastries, cakes, biscuits, and strawberries and cream when available. In winter, tea time is a cosy affair, perhaps around the fireside, with hot buttered toast, crumpets, muffins, teacakes, fruit cake and tea breads spread with butter and honey or home-made jam.

The main part of this book gives recipes for all the traditional British tea time foods: breads and tea breads, sandwiches, scones, biscuits, cakes, savouries and jams. Recipes are also given for special occasions: a children's tea party, a Valentine's Day tea, a Hallowe'en tea, an ice cream tea and an elegant celebration tea. Hints on presentation and serving are given throughout.

DRINKING TEA

Here is everything you need to know to enjoy that essential tea time beverage, tea. The various types are listed below, as well as the definitive method of making the perfect cup of tea, and also all the different pieces of equipment for making and serving tea. Finally, some delicious suggestions are given for tea-based drinks, including an iced tea and summer tea punch for hot weather, and a potent brandy warmer for winter.

♦ TYPES OF TEA ♦

There are three main types of tea to choose from: black tea, oolong or red tea, and green tea. Each type of tea has a number of varieties, each with its own distinctive flavour and aroma. The main varieties are described here. Some teas are considered particularly suitable for drinking at certain times of the day, and guidelines are given for this as well as recommendations for serving with or without milk. Experiment with the different types of tea until you find the one that you like best.

Loose leaf tea is generally considered to have the best flavour, because it contains larger leaves, which give a better flavour although needing longer to brew. Tea-bags usually contain the finest siftings and broken leaves of tea, giving a stronger, darker liquid which needs very little time to brew. However, there are many good quality tea-bags now available, with many speciality teas to choose from.

BLACK TEA

The leaves of black tea are dried after plucking and then machine-rolled and oxidized (or 'fermented' in the tea trade), when they turn a bright coppery colour because of the absorption of oxygen. After oxidization, the leaves are dried in hot air chambers. During this stage the leaves turn black and the sugars in the tea are caramelized, giving the slightly burnt aroma that distinguishes black tea from oolong tea or green tea.

Black tea is higher in caffeine than oolong or green tea, but the level is still significantly lower than that of coffee. In Britain, black teas are usually drunk with milk, but some of the more delicate China teas such as Lapsang Souchong and Yunnan are very drinkable without.

The best known black teas:

Assam From north-east India, this tea has brittle, blackish leaves which give a reddish tea with a brisk, strong flavour. It is an ideal breakfast and early morning tea. Serve with milk or lemon.

Ceylon Best quality or 'high-grown' Ceylon tea is considered one of the best teas in the world. It has a golden colour, full taste and delicate fragrance, suitable for any time of the day. Serve with milk or lemon.

China Caravan This is a fine blend of Keemun teas. The name comes from the fact that it came by camel along the Caravan route from China. It gives a clear liquor with a smooth taste.

Darjeeling This is grown in West Bengal in the foothills of the Himalayas, and is often called the champagne of tea. It has a rich flavour and fine bouquet reminiscent of Muscatel. Darjeeling can be served throughout the day and is suitable as an after-dinner tea.

Earl Grey This tea is named after the nineteenth-century British statesman the Second Earl Grey, who was given the recipe as a result of a diplomatic mission to China. The tea is a blend of China teas mixed with oil of bergamot. Because of its delicate flavour it is best drunk without milk or sugar. It is an ideal afternoon tea.

English Breakfast This is usually a blend of Indian and Ceylon teas, with a strong, full-bodied, brisk flavour. It is best served with milk and, as its name implies, is an ideal early morning drink.

Irish Breakfast Usually a blend of strong Assam teas with a good flavour. It is a breakfast or early morning tea, usually drunk with milk.

Keemun A fine quality China tea from Anhui Province. It gives a fragrant light-coloured clear liquor, with a smooth, slightly nutty, sweet taste. Drink with or without milk in the afternoon or evening.

Kenya High-grown Kenyan tea is a highly respected tea. It has a fine flavour and gives a deep reddish-gold liquor, suitable for any time of day. Kenya tea is usually drunk with milk.

Lapsang Souchong The best quality Lapsang Souchong is from Fujian Province in China and has a very distinctive smoky aroma and flavour. It is best drunk without milk but perhaps with a slice of lemon. It is an ideal summer and outdoor tea, popular in the afternoon and early evening.

Orange Pekoe The term 'Pekoe' or 'Orange Pekoe' is actually used to denote leaf size. Pekoe from *Pak-ho*, meaning white hair in Chinese, refers to the whiteness under the leaf. It can be used for any tea, for instance Assam Orange Pekoe or Darjeeling Orange Pekoe. However, people have come to think of Orange Pekoe as a tea in its own right, and it is usually sold today as a highly scented Souchong. It is often blended with Jasmine tea to add flavour.

Rose Pouchong This is from Guangdong, further down from Fujian on the south-east coast of China. Rose petals are mixed with the leaves and the resulting flavour is very delicate.

Russian This is often called Georgian tea because it is cultivated in the Republic of Georgia in Russia. It has a fairly flat flavour which can be improved by serving with a slice of lemon.

Yunnan From China's remote western province of Yunnan, this tea has only recently become available to the world market. It has a sweet aroma and gives a clear, bright delicate liquor. Drink without milk, perhaps with a slice of lemon.

OOLONG (RED) TEA

Oolong teas are produced in a number of provinces in China and the best come mainly from Fujian on the south-east coast of China, and also from Taiwan. After picking, the tea is processed in the same way as black tea but the oxidization period is much shorter. Because of this the flavour and colour of oolong tea is mid-way between that of black tea and green tea.

Oolong teas have a low caffeine content and are best served without milk or sugar but perhaps with lemon.

The best known oolong teas:

Formosa/China Oolong This tea has a large greenish-brown leaf, the very best having silver tips. It has a light, slightly peachy flavour and produces a straw-coloured liquor. It is best served without milk and is an ideal afternoon or evening tea.

Formosa/China Pouchong China Pouchong has a brighter taste than Formosa Pouchong. The leaves are scented with gardenia, jasmine or yulan blossom, and the tea is pale pinky-brown with a mild flavour. Serve in the afternoon or evening, perhaps with a slice of lemon.

GREEN TEA

The best green tea comes from Zhejiang Province on the east coast of China. After picking, the leaves are first steamed to prevent fermentation. They are then machine-rolled and fired under a current of hot air to give green-grey pellets.

All green teas have a low caffeine content. They are best served without milk, either plain or with lemon and sugar. Green teas are best served quite weak, but experiment to find the strength you prefer.

The best known green teas:

Gunpowder This is from Zhejiang Province. It is said that when the British first arrived in China and were shown the pellets of green tea they nicknamed it gunpowder because of its resemblance to the grey lead ball shot. Gunpowder tea is the most popular of the green teas in the West, and produces a delicate, straw-coloured liquor with a penetrating taste. It is best drunk in the afternoon or evening.

Jasmine From Fujian Province, this is a green or a blend of green and black teas mixed with jasmine flowers. It has a very distinctive, delicate flavour. Serve in the afternoon or evening, preferably plain but with lemon if preferred.

SCENTED AND FLAVOURED TEAS

There is a growing interest in scented and flavoured teas and many varieties are now available. Scented and flavoured teas are usually a blend of teas mixed with dried fruits or flowers for added flavour. Jasmine tea is probably the best known scented tea in the East and Earl Grey probably the best known in the West. Scented and flavoured teas are suitable for any time of the day and are best drunk without milk or sugar. Experiment with infusing times to find the strength of tea you prefer.

Scented and flavoured teas include: apple, blackcurrant, cherry, cinnamon and spice, fruit and spice, lemon, lime, mandarin, mint, nutmeg and cinnamon, spice, spiced apple and vanilla.

INFUSIONS AND TISANES

Infusions or tisanes are drinks brewed from various leaves, roots, seeds, flowers, fruits and herbs other than the tea bush and are sometimes called herb teas, although strictly the name tea only applies to drinks made from the tea bush. Infusions are popular because they are refreshing and caffeine-free, and because of the particular properties that each possesses.

Infusions are best served quite weak, and without milk. They are usually taken without sugar but a little sweetener can be added if desired.

The best known infusions are:

Burdock A purifier of the blood and cure for skin diseases.

Camomile Said to ease aches and pains and to induce sleep.

Elderflower A traditional remedy for gout and thought to soothe the nerves.

Ginseng Thought to be a remedy for impotence.

Lime Blossom Said to alleviate headaches and colds.

Rosehip A popular, delicate brew usually blended with hibiscus.

Rosemary Thought to stimulate the memory.

Sage A remedy for sore throats and a lost voice.

♦ HOW TO MAKE A PERFECT CUP OF TEA ♦

It is pleasing to find that more and more people are again interested in the finer points of tea drinking and are not content to make do with mugs and tea-bags. Tea really is the most refreshing drink in the middle of the afternoon and it is a shame to spoil its flavour by not brewing it correctly.

To make a perfect cup of tea, first fill the kettle with fresh water. Warm a clean teapot by swilling it with hot water and then pour the water out. Place in the teapot one teaspoonful of tea per person and one extra 'for the pot'. When the water is boiling, take the teapot to the kettle and pour the boiling water on to the tea. Place the lid on the pot and leave to brew for 3–5 minutes. Stir before pouring.

To serve tea, first pour a little milk, if required, into the cup and then pour in the tea through a strainer. This habit of pouring the milk into the cup before the tea dates back to the late seventeenth century. Until then the British had only known pewter and earthenware mugs for drinking ale, and were afraid that hot tea poured into the newly introduced fine porcelain cups would crack them unless milk was poured in first. Whether you do the same is a matter of personal taste, although if the milk is poured in first it will blend in more readily with the tea.

Although tea should not really be sweetened, sugar should always be supplied in case guests require it. The sugar should traditionally be white, either cube or granulated, although some people do prefer brown.

♦ TEA-MAKING EQUIPMENT ♦

TEA CADDIES

A caddy is a small container used for storing tea. The word originates from the word *cathy*, an oriental measure for weighing tea. In the mid-seventeenth century caddies were lockable, and the tea was kept in them to stop servants from pilfering the very expensive leaves. It was in fact customary for the tea to be brewed for tea parties by the lady of the house herself, rather than letting the servants do it.

It is vital that tea be kept in airtight containers. Tea-bags should be transferred from their packet to a caddy as they will dry out and taste stale very quickly if left open to the air. Loose tea will keep for up to 2 years in an unopened, airtight container. Tea-bags will only last for about 6 months.

TEAPOTS

Teapots were first brought to Europe from China in the early seventeenth century. Made from china, they were generally broad and squat with wide spouts that would not clog with tea leaves. They were quite small, not because tea was so expensive, but so that each person could have his or her own pot.

During the eighteenth century, the spouts on teapots became more tapered and curved, and the body of the pot became a more elegant pear shape. Nowadays teapots are available in all sorts of shapes, sizes and designs; and can be made from china, pottery, porcelain, stainless steel, glass and silver. A teapot made from almost any material will make good tea. Aluminium should be avoided, however, as it gives the tea a blue tinge, and enamel should not be used if it is chipped as metals can leak into the tea.

Do not wash the teapot in detergent or soap as the lingering taste will spoil the tea. To remove tannin, soak the pot for several hours with 20 ml (4 tsp) bicarbonate of soda (baking soda) dissolved in hot water. However, if the teapot has been washed with detergent or soap powder it can be sweetened ready for use by placing a spoonful of dry tea leaves inside the pot and leaving for a few days.

How to choose a teapot:

1 Make quite sure that the teapot can be picked up comfortably by the handle without your knuckles touching the side of the pot. If this is not possible your fingers will be badly burned during pouring.

2 Choose a teapot with a hole in the lid. This allows air to enter the pot as the tea is being poured and therefore prevents dribbling from the spout.

3 There should be a lug (a small projection) on the lid to prevent it from falling off during pouring.

4 Inspect the inside of the teapot to ensure that the glaze is good. A badly finished glaze will affect the flavour of the tea.

5 An extra feature to look for is holes at the base of the spout to catch tea leaves.

INFUSERS

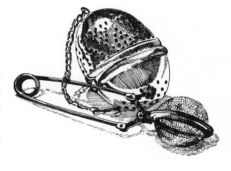

There are many stainless steel mesh infusers available. Tea leaves are put into the infuser, which is then placed inside the teapot. Their advantage is that the tea leaves can be removed from the water once the required strength has been reached, which stops the tea from stewing. It is important that the infuser is large enough to allow the tea leaves to expand and therefore give a good brew.

TEA STRAINERS

The strainer spoon had become a standard part of tea equipment by the late seventeenth century. It was used to convey tea from the caddy to the pot, therefore sifting out unwanted dust and leaving only the larger, better quality leaves. The strainer was also used to remove impurities from the surface of the tea in the cup, and it often had a spike in the handle which was used to unblock the perforations at the base of the spout of the teapot, where tea leaves collected.

Nowadays, tea strainers are bowl-shaped with a handle, designed to be placed over the cup while the brewed tea is

poured through. Tea strainers are essential when using loose tea without an infuser, if the tea leaves are not to end up in the cup. The English actually do not mind a few leaves in their tea, but the Americans abhor this happening. It is well worth scouring antique and junk markets for strainers as it is still possible to find elegant and stylish ones from the 1920s and 1930s, made from silver, silver plate, porcelain or chrome, at very reasonable prices.

TEA COSIES

Tea cosies are padded teapot covers, and should only be used if the tea is being made with tea-bags or an infuser. Once the tea has reached the required strength the tea-bag or infuser can be removed and the cosy used to keep the brew warm. If, however, the cosy is placed over a teapot containing loose leaves, the water will stay hot for longer and overdraw the tea, giving a stewed taste.

TEACUPS

The teacups first imported from China (and still used by the Chinese today) were tiny bowls, about 5 centimetres (2 inches) high, holding little more than a few thimblefuls of tea. The idea of adding a handle came from the English 'posset' cup, which was used for hot drinks. As the English pottery and porcelain industry grew, teacups were made with handles and gradually became larger in size.

MILK JUGS AND CREAMERS

Early milk jugs used for tea were often shaped like a cow, with a hole in the middle of the back to pour in the milk and a spout in the mouth from where the milk was poured into the teacup. These early jugs were usually made from silver or porcelain. Nowadays, small and rather plainer jugs and creamers are generally used, but there is a wide variety to choose from.

Types of tea A selection of loose leaf teas, including black, oolong and green varieties. See pages 9–12 for details of each tea.

Gunpowder

Earl Grey

Lapsang Souchong

Ceylon

Jasmine

Darjeeling

Keemun

China Oolong

Rose Pouchong

SUGAR BOWLS AND TONGS

Sugar bowls are a pretty addition to a tea table, with sugar tongs for lump or cube sugar or a small spoon if loose. Sugar tongs were developed in the late seventeenth century, and were first shaped like scissors with a sharp edge for breaking off pieces from the large loaf of sugar. These early tongs also often had a screw-in spike at one end, used for unblocking the spout of the teapot.

LEMON SQUEEZERS

If you use a lot of lemon in your tea, a squeezer is a very useful item. Fresh lemon juice can be added cleanly, avoiding wet and sticky fingers. The squeezer is made like a metal claw into which a wedge of lemon is placed. The perforations in one side of the claw allow the lemon juice to be squeezed into the cup without any pips and skin escaping. Wedges of lemon should be served in a bowl ready on the tea table.

TEASPOONS

Teaspoons began to appear in the late seventeenth century as the practice of sweetening tea grew. At this time spoons used for tea and coffee were the same size. By the eighteenth century teaspoons had become slightly larger than coffee spoons, and today they are about twice the size. Teaspoons are often found in boxed sets of 6, with a pair of sugar tongs.

◆ TEA-BASED DRINKS ◆

BRANDY WARMER

Add 15 ml (1 tbsp) of brandy to a cup of hot English Breakfast tea. Float a slice of orange or lemon on top and add a cinnamon stick. Whisky may be used instead of brandy in the same way.

Afternoon tea Clockwise from top: Asparagus & ham sandwiches (see page 37); Cucumber sandwiches (see page 40); Scones (see page 49); Lemon meringue fingers (see page 65); Frangipani tarts (see page 64).

EASTERN PROMISE

Place 575 ml (1 pt) cold Jasmine tea in a jug with 30 ml (2 tbsp) undiluted orange squash. Add the juice from a 227 g (8 oz) can of pineapple slices and 275 ml ($\frac{1}{2}$ pt) bitter lemon. Stir in some crushed ice and garnish with the pineapple slices and a few orange slices.

ICED TEA

This must be made with Ceylon Breakfast tea, which has the property of remaining crystal clear when cold.

Make a pot of tea, adding one extra spoonful of leaves than would normally be used. Place a little sugar in a large jug and fill the jug with ice cubes. Strain the tea through a tea strainer into the jug and top up with cold water. Chill for several hours. To serve, pour into glasses and garnish with slices of lemon or a few bruised mint or sage leaves.

SCOTCH MIST

This should be served in the evening. Mix together in a saucepan 3 parts Ceylon tea to 2 parts whisky. Add honey to taste. Heat through, but do not boil. Pour into small coffee cups and float a little cream on top.

SUMMER TEA PUNCH

Mix together 575 ml (1 pt) cold Darjeeling tea, 225 g (8 oz) caster sugar, 150 ml ($\frac{1}{4}$ pt) rum and a 411 g (14$\frac{1}{2}$ oz) can of pineapple cubes. Chill for at least 2 hours. Pour into a large bowl with ice cubes and add 1 bottle of dry white wine and 1 ltr (1$\frac{3}{4}$ pt) lemonade. Garnish with orange and lemon slices and maraschino cherries.

HOW TO USE THE RECIPES

The recipes in this book have easy-to-follow instructions and have all been tested at least twice to ensure the very best results. When using the recipes, it is important to measure the ingredients precisely and to use the correct baking equipment.

Listed below is a glossary of the basic equipment, cooking terms and methods used in the book. Some useful hints for cooking cakes are also included.

Both metric and imperial measurements are given in the recipes: use either, but do not combine the two.

All fruit and vegetables should be wiped or washed before using; and peeled, topped and tailed as necessary.

The amounts of seasonings and spices can be adjusted in most recipes to suit personal tastes if desired.

◆ SUGGESTED EQUIPMENT ◆

Baking Tins Strong easy-clean tins are best. For basic cake cookery you will need:

Loaf tins The most common sizes are 450 g (1 lb) and 900 g (2 lb).

Round deep tins The most useful sizes are 18 cm (7 in), 20 cm (8 in), 23 cm (9 in) and 25.5 cm (10 in). It is also useful if these tins are spring-release, particularly for very soft cakes.

Sandwich tins Buy these in pairs; 18 cm (7 in) and 20 cm (8 in) round are the most useful.

Small patty tins These are essential for small cakes and tarts. Different widths, depths and shapes are available.

Square deep tins The most useful sizes are 15 cm (6 in), 18 cm (7 in) and 20 cm (8 in).

Swiss roll tins The most common size is 28 × 18 cm (11 × 7 in), but it is also useful to have a slightly larger size, 33 × 23 cm (13 × 9 in).

Baking Trays 2 or more flat metal baking trays are useful for biscuits, teacakes, muffins, bread rolls, etc.

Beater A hand-held rotary or electric beater, or the beater attachment of a food mixer, is suitable for most of the beating and whipping processes in this book.

Bowls It is useful to have a selection of bowls of varying sizes for mixing. They can be made from plastic, glass, pottery or porcelain. Ovenproof bowls are particularly useful.

Dredger This is not essential but is useful for shaking sugar and flour over cakes, biscuits, pies and rolls.

Grater A fine grater is needed for removing the rind and zest of oranges and lemons.

Knives A selection of knives is needed, to include one with a sharp, serrated blade for cutting fruit, etc., and a round-bladed one for mixing pastry.

Litre or Pint Measure The best kind is a jug with a good spout, which holds 1 litre ($1\frac{3}{4}$ pints) or more. It should be clearly marked in both metric and imperial, and be transparent enough to see the contents, and be heat-resistant.

Palette Knife This is used for smoothing the tops of cakes, spreading icings, and lifting biscuits and other items off baking trays. It needs to have a firm, wide blade.

Pastry Brush This is used to brush glazes over pastries, biscuits, tarts and bakes.

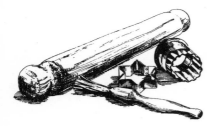

Pastry Cutters Basic cutters measuring 4 cm ($1\frac{1}{2}$ in), 5 cm (2 in), 6 cm ($2\frac{1}{2}$ in) and 7.5 cm (3 in) are needed. Other shapes and sizes can be used for most biscuits and canapés as desired.

Piping or Forcing Bag For decorative application of icings, cream and other fillings or toppings. A nylon or plastic bag is best as it is easy to wash. A variety of piping nozzles are available, the most basic of which are a star, a fine nozzle for lettering and marbling effects, and a 1 cm ($\frac{1}{2}$ in) nozzle.

Preserving Pan This is essential for making jams and pickles. Aluminium and stainless steel pans are best.

Rolling Pin A good heavy wooden pin with a good smooth surface is best. Glass ones which can be filled with cold or iced water are also good, as they help to keep the temperature of the pastry down.

Scales The choice of kitchen scales is very much one of personal preference. Do always check, however, that the needle is exactly on zero before you start weighing ingredients.

Sieve or Strainer A wire sieve or strainer is very useful as it is firm enough to purée soft fruit as well as to sift flour and icing sugar.

Slotted Spoon This is needed for lifting and draining fried foods such as doughnuts or beignets from hot oil.

Spatula or Scraper The best are made from pliable rubber and have a very fine edge that enables you to scrape all the mixture from a bowl or pan.

Spoon Measures It is a good idea to buy proper spoon measures and not to rely on everyday tablespoons and teaspoons, as these do not always hold exactly 15 ml or 5 ml and accurate measuring of ingredients is vital for baking.

Wire Cooling Rack It is essential to transfer cakes and biscuits from the baking tray or tin on to a wire rack to allow cool air to circulate around them. Cakes in particular will become soggy and heavy if placed on a solid surface to cool.

Wooden Spoons It is useful to have a collection of wooden spoons for stirring and beating, in a variety of sizes and weights.

◆ COOKING TERMS ◆

Beat To mix ingredients together by turning over and over quickly to incorporate as much air as possible. This can be done with a wooden spoon, a fork or a whisk. For cake-making purposes a hand–held electric beater or a food mixer is best, particularly if making cake mixtures in large quantities.

To 'beat until the mixture leaves a trail' means that the correct consistency should be tested by lifting the beater and allowing some of the mixture to run off. If this immediately sinks back into the rest of the mixture, it is not ready. When it sits on the surface making a visible trail, it is ready.

Dredge This is usually done with flour or sugar and means to coat the surface of the food item (for example a loaf, biscuit or cake) with the dry ingredient.

Fold in To mix one ingredient into another without affecting the air content that has already been beaten in. Usually sugar is folded into egg white, or flour into beaten fat, sugar and egg. Always fold the lighter ingredients or mixtures into the heavier ones.

To fold in successfully, use a metal spoon or spatula. Cut through the mixture and lift, carefully bringing the spoon or spatula up and over in a circular, slicing movement.

Glaze This means to coat the surface of a food before, during or after cooking, to improve the appearance or give a sticky surface for another ingredient to adhere to. Glazing is usually done lightly with a pastry brush.

Knead This is done with the fingers and palms of your hands and helps give a dough the required smoothness and consistency. The kneading process is vital as it strengthens and develops the gluten in the flour, which helps the dough to rise.

Cover a board or firm surface with 50–75 g (2–3 oz) flour, place the dough on this and sprinkle a little more flour on top. Using your fingers, fold the dough towards you, then push down and away with the palms of your hands. Rotate the dough slightly and repeat. Do this for about 10 minutes until the dough feels smooth, elastic and not sticky.

Line Small patty tins and loaf tins which are to be used for bread only need to be greased, but for most other cakes the tin should be lined and then greased.

To line a tin, first grease the entire inside surface, making quite sure that every part is coated. Cut out a piece of greaseproof paper or baking parchment to fit the bottom of the tin. It must be an exact fit, or it will spoil the shape of the cake.

Measure the circumference of the tin and cut out a strip of greaseproof paper or baking parchment long enough to go round the tin and overlap slightly, and wide enough to stand approx. 5 cm (2 in) higher than the tin. If the tin is round, snip one long edge of the paper with diagonal cuts so that it will ease into the tin. This is not necessary for a square tin.

Place the strip inside the tin and fit carefully against the piece of paper in the base. Grease the lined tin well so that the entire inside surface is coated with a thin layer.

To line a Swiss roll tin, cut out a piece of greaseproof paper or baking parchment just big enough to line the base and sides. Do not have the paper standing up higher than the edge of the tin, as this may stop the cake from browning.

Line with pastry To line a flan ring or dish with pastry, roll out the pastry into a circle about 2.5 cm (1 in) larger than the ring. Using the rolling pin, lift the pastry on to the ring. Press the pastry into the sides, pressing into the gaps with your fingers if the ring is fluted. Trim off the excess pastry with a knife, allowing a little for shrinkage during cooking.

Melt Some cakes, particularly those made with eggs, require you to melt the fats, sugar, syrup, etc., before adding the dry ingredients. The temperature should be carefully controlled so that the ingredients only warm through gently and do not boil.

Pipe Soft mixtures, doughs and icings can be forced through a special piping or pastry bag to give a controlled shape or decoration. Meringues, éclairs, shortcakes and cake icing are usually piped.

Roll out When rolling out pastry, place it on a lightly floured board and use a floured rolling pin. Roll lightly and evenly with short strokes, in one direction only, rotating the pastry frequently to keep an even shape. Make sure that the pastry does not stick to the board, but do not turn it over or it will absorb too much flour from the board.

Rub or cut in To mix in fat with flour and/or other dry ingredients. This is done either with the fingertips or with a round-bladed knife or a pastry blender. The action should be light and quick, and the fat must be evenly distributed through the flour so that there are no large lumps. Shortbread, pastry and biscuit recipes often start with this method.

Whip To beat as much air as possible into ingredients or substances such as egg white or cream, to give a light, fluffy texture and increased volume. It is best done with a balloon whisk or electric beater.

◆ CAKE COOKING HINTS ◆

1 Choose the right equipment and utensils.

2 Always heat the oven to the required temperature 15 minutes before the cake is due to go in, if possible. If the oven is not hot enough when the cake goes in, it may not rise properly.

3 Put the cake straight into the oven as soon as it is ready or the air beaten into it during preparation will be lost.

4 Do not open the oven door until after at least three-quarters of the cooking time. Until the cake has set the temperature must remain high and constant, or the cake may collapse.

5 As a general guideline, unless otherwise stated in the recipe, place small cakes, scones and Swiss rolls slightly above the middle of the oven; place sponge cakes, sponge sandwiches, tea breads, light fruit cakes, biscuits and shortbreads in the middle of the oven, and place richer fruit cakes slightly below the middle of the oven.

6 To test when the cake is cooked, use the following methods:
For sponges and sandwich cakes, press lightly with a finger. If cooked, the sponge will spring back.
For fruit cakes, tea breads and loaves, push a clean, dry skewer into the middle of the cake. If it comes out clean, the cake is ready.
Small cakes are well risen, golden brown and firm when cooked.
If the cakes are not ready, return to the oven and if necessary lower the temperature so that the cake will cook without overbrowning. Cook for a further 15–20 minutes and then test again.

✦ IF THINGS GO WRONG ✦

If you follow the recipes carefully and use the exact amounts of ingredients and correct tins, you should achieve perfect results every time. If, however, the cake is not as successful as you hoped, the following checklist may be helpful when you come to try again.

Cake risen too much in the middle This could mean that there was too much raising agent, not enough beating of the mixture or that the oven was too hot.

Cake sunk in the middle This is most common with fruit cakes. It can mean that there was not enough beating of the fat and sugar, that there was not enough raising agent or that the oven was too cool.

Coarse texture to the cake This probably means that there was not enough beating, or not enough flour. It could also mean that the oven was too cool.

Cracked top to the cake The tin was probably too small or the oven too hot. It could also mean that too much raising agent or flour was added to the mixture.

Fruit sunk to the bottom of the cake This is probably because there was not enough beating of the fat and sugar, or that the mixture was made too soft by too much liquid. Try tossing the fruit in flour before adding to the mixture.

Hard outside but soggy in the middle This is most common with fruit cakes or sponges. The oven may have been too hot or the cake positioned too high in the oven. It could also mean that there was too much liquid or too much fat (or similar melted liquids, such as syrup). Place a circle of brown paper or a double layer of greaseproof paper or baking parchment over the top of the cake, with a hole to let the steam out in the middle.

Heavy texture to the cake This probably means that there was too much fat or sugar in the mixture, or not enough flour or raising agent. It could also mean that there was not enough beating, or that the oven was too cool.

Large holes in the cake This may mean that too much raising agent was used.

THE
RECIPES

BREADS & TEA BREADS

Home-made bread tastes so different and so much nicer than anything generally available in the shops that it is well worth all the time and effort involved. Serve it at tea time, sliced and buttered on its own, or use for sandwiches (see pages 35–43). Many delicious bread recipes are given in this chapter, including oat bread and yogurt rye bread as well as plain white and wholewheat. To give a crisp crust to a loaf, lightly beaten egg white can be brushed over when it is nearly cooked. To give a soft crust, brush the loaf with melted butter when nearly cooked.

Tea breads are always a welcome addition to the tea table, and can be eaten plain or spread with butter and preserves. The selection here includes a number of traditional recipes from different parts of the country, as well as some old family favourites. Many of the recipes require dried fruit (raisins, currants and sultanas), and you should make sure that the fruit is as moist as possible. For the best results, try soaking it in a little sherry for an hour before use.

INGREDIENTS

150 g (5 oz) margarine,
  softened, plus 5 ml (1 tsp)
  to grease tin
150 g (5 oz) caster sugar
3 medium eggs, beaten
4 ripe bananas, mashed
¼ tsp vanilla essence
400 g (14 oz) plain
  wholewheat flour, sifted
100 g (4 oz) ground almonds
10 ml (2 tsp) baking powder
¼ tsp salt
30 ml (2 tbsp) demerara sugar

ALMOND BANANA TEA
♦ BREAD ♦

This loaf combines the subtle flavour of almonds and the sweetness and moistness of bananas. It is best made with over-ripe bananas, which you can buy cheaply from the greengrocer.

♦ **Preparation** 20 minutes ♦ **Cooking** 1¼–1½ hours ♦ **Makes** 18 cm (7 in) square loaf ♦

METHOD

Heat the oven to 350°F (180°C/Gas 4) and grease and line an 18 cm (7 in) square tin.

Cream the margarine and sugar together and beat thoroughly until light and fluffy. Beat the eggs gradually into the mixture, beating hard between each addition. Mix the mashed bananas with the vanilla and stir into the mixture. Do not worry if it curdles, as this will not spoil the cake. Beat really well to incorporate air into the mixture.

Combine the flour, almonds, baking powder and salt in a separate bowl and fold into the banana mixture. Blend thoroughly. Spoon into the prepared tin and sprinkle the demerara sugar over the top.

Bake for 1¼–1½ hours until firm. Test with a skewer and, if cooked, remove from the oven and turn out on to a wire rack to cool. Wrap in foil and leave for at least 1 day before eating.

◆ BARA BRITH ◆

This is a traditional Welsh tea bread and recipes vary depending on which part of Wales you are in. Some people like it fairly dry and in other regions it is a much moister, spicier cake. I prefer this moist version, which is good with or without butter.

◆ **Preparation** 2–2½ hours ◆ **Cooking** 20–30 minutes ◆ **Makes** 900 g (2 lb) loaf ◆

INGREDIENTS
450 g (1 lb) plain flour, sifted
5 ml (1 tsp) salt
150 ml (¼ pt) milk, plus
    15–30 ml (1–2 tbsp) extra
    if necessary
15 g (½ oz) fresh yeast
75 g (3 oz) butter, plus 5 ml
    (1 tsp) to grease tin
100 g (4 oz) each of
    sultanas, raisins and
    currants
75 g (3 oz) soft brown sugar
50 g (2 oz) mixed candied peel
10 ml (2 tsp) ground mixed
    spice

Pictured opposite page 32

METHOD
Heat the oven to 275°F (140°C/Gas 1). Put the flour and salt in an ovenproof bowl and warm in the oven for a few minutes.

Warm the milk in a saucepan and pour half of it on to the yeast in a bowl, blending with a fork to form a paste. Pour the creamed yeast on to the warmed flour and mix well with a fork. Melt the butter with the remaining milk and add to the flour, mixing to a light dough, and adding a little more warm milk if the dough is too dry.

Leave the dough in the bowl, cover with a damp cloth and leave to rise in a warm place until doubled in size. This should take 35–40 minutes at normal room temperature.

Grease a 900 g (2 lb) loaf tin and place in the oven to warm. Put the dried fruit, sugar, candied peel and spice in an ovenproof bowl and warm in the oven for a few minutes. Then, using your hands, knead the fruit into the dough in the bowl so that it is evenly distributed. If the dough becomes too stiff add a little more warm milk.

Shape the dough and place it in the warmed tin. Cover with a light cloth and leave in a warm place until the dough has risen to the top of the tin. This should take about 1–1½ hours. Heat the oven to 400°F (200°C/Gas 6).

Bake the loaf for 20–30 minutes. For the last 10 minutes of cooking, cover the top of the loaf with foil. Test with a skewer and, when firm, remove from the oven and leave to cool in the tin before turning out on to a wire rack to cool completely.

INGREDIENTS

450 g (1 lb) mixed dried fruit
(raisins, currants, sultanas,
candied peel and cherries)
200 g (7 oz) soft brown sugar
275 ml (½ pt) cold black tea
5 ml (1 tsp) margarine, to
grease tin
2 medium eggs, beaten
250 g (9 oz) self-raising flour,
sifted
Good pinch of salt
5 ml (1 tsp) ground mixed
spice

◆ BARMBRACK ◆

*This is a traditional Irish fruit bread which can be eaten as it is or sliced
and spread with butter.*

◆ **Preparation** 3 hours or overnight to soak fruit, plus 10–15 minutes ◆
◆ **Cooking** 1½–1¾ hours ◆ **Makes** 900 g (2 lb) loaf ◆

METHOD

Soak the dried fruit and sugar in the tea for at least 3 hours, or, if
possible, overnight.

Heat the oven to 350°F (180°C/Gas 4) and grease and line a 900 g
(2 lb) loaf tin.

Mix the eggs, flour, salt and spice into the fruit and tea mixture, and
beat well. Pour into the prepared tin.

Bake for 1½–1¾ hours or until a skewer comes out clean. Remove
from the oven and leave to cool in the tin for 5–10 minutes before
turning out on to a wire rack to cool completely. Wrap in foil to stop it
from drying.

INGREDIENTS

450 g (1 lb) mixed dried fruit
(raisins, currants, sultanas,
candied peel and cherries)
275 ml (½ pt) sweet cider
5 ml (1 tsp) margarine, to
grease tin
275 g (10 oz) self-raising flour,
sifted
50 g (2 oz) chopped walnuts
or almonds
175 g (6 oz) soft brown sugar
Grated rind of 1 orange
Grated rind of 1 lemon
2 medium eating apples,
peeled, cored and grated
2 large eggs, beaten

◆ CIDER LOAF ◆

If you find this loaf too moist, add 25 g (1 oz) extra flour to the dough.

◆ **Preparation** 3 hours or overnight to soak fruit, plus 20 minutes ◆
◆ **Cooking** 1½–1¾ hours ◆ **Makes** 20 cm (8 in) square loaf ◆

METHOD

Soak the dried fruit in the cider in a saucepan for at least 3 hours, or, if
possible, overnight.

Heat the oven to 325°F (170°C/Gas 3) and grease and line a 20 cm
(8 in) square tin.

Bring the cider and fruit to the boil in the saucepan, remove from the
heat and allow to cool. Mix together the flour, nuts, sugar, orange and
lemon rind and grated apple in a bowl. Gradually add the cider mixture
and the beaten eggs, mixing in thoroughly.

Turn into the prepared tin and bake for 1½–1¾ hours until well risen,
golden brown and firm to the touch. Remove from the oven and turn
out on to a wire rack to cool.

CREAM CHEESE LOAF
♦ WITH CHIVES ♦

This bread is delicious served warm and buttered, and is also good toasted. If fresh chives are not available, use 15 ml (1 tbsp) dried instead.

♦ **Preparation** 2–2¼ hours ♦ **Cooking** 45–50 minutes ♦ **Makes** 900 g (2 lb) loaf ♦

METHOD

Stir the yeast into the warm water until dissolved. Add the malt extract and stir well to blend thoroughly. Leave in a warm place for 15–20 minutes until frothy.

Mix the flour, onion salt, chives, cream cheese and milk together. Beat with a fork until well blended, creamy and smooth. Gradually pour in the yeast mixture and mix with a fork to form a soft dough.

Turn on to a floured board and knead for about 10 minutes until smooth and elastic. Replace in the bowl and cover with a damp cloth. Leave in a warm place to rise for about 1 hour.

Oil a 900 g (2 lb) loaf tin. Turn the dough on to the floured board and knead again for a few minutes. Shape the dough and place in the prepared tin. Cover with a damp cloth and leave in a warm place until the dough has risen to the top of the tin. This should take 35–40 minutes. Meanwhile, heat the oven to 400°F (200°C/Gas 6).

Bake the loaf for 10 minutes. Then, reduce the heat to 350°F (180°C/Gas 4) and bake for a further 35–40 minutes until the loaf is lightly browned on top and sounds hollow when tapped on the bottom. Turn out on to a wire rack to cool.

INGREDIENTS

25 g (1 oz) fresh yeast
200 ml (7 fl oz) warm water
10 ml (2 tsp) malt extract
450 g (1 lb) plain wholewheat flour, sifted, plus 50–75 g (2–3 oz) to flour board
10 ml (2 tsp) onion salt
30 ml (2 tbsp) finely chopped fresh chives
175 g (6 oz) cream cheese
30 ml (2 tbsp) milk
5 ml (1 tsp) oil, to grease tin

♦ FIG LOAF ♦

This loaf has a coarse, moist texture, and the subtle sweetness of figs.

♦ **Preparation** 1 hour to soak figs, plus 10–15 minutes ♦ **Cooking** 1¼–1½ hours ♦
♦ **Makes** 900 g (2 lb) loaf ♦

METHOD

Place the figs, tea, sugar and treacle in a bowl and leave for at least 1 hour (the longer the better).

Heat the oven to 350°F (180°C/Gas 4) and grease and line a 900 g (2 lb) loaf tin.

Mix the remaining ingredients together and fold into the fig mixture. Beat with a wooden spoon until well blended and pour into the tin.

Bake for 1¼–1½ hours or until a skewer comes out clean. Remove from the oven and leave to cool in the tin for 5–10 minutes before turning out on to a wire rack to cool completely.

INGREDIENTS

225 g (8 oz) dried figs, chopped
175 ml (6 fl oz) cold black tea
100 g (4 oz) soft brown sugar
15 ml (1 tbsp) black treacle
5 ml (1 tsp) margarine, to grease tin
225 g (8 oz) plain wholewheat flour, sifted
20 ml (4 tsp) baking powder
1 medium egg, beaten

Pictured opposite page 32

INGREDIENTS

15 g (½ oz) fresh yeast

275 ml (½ pt) warm water

450 g (1 lb) granary or malt-blend flour, sifted, plus 50–75 g (2–3 oz) to flour board

5 ml (1 tsp) salt

15 ml (1 tbsp) malt extract

15 ml (1 tbsp) sunflower oil, plus 10 ml (2 tsp) to grease bowl and baking tray

◆ GRANARY BREAD ◆

This popular bread has a nutty taste and grainy texture, and is ideal for sandwiches and toasting.

◆ **Preparation** 2½–3 hours ◆ **Cooking** 35–40 minutes ◆ **Makes** 900 g (2 lb) loaf ◆

METHOD

Stir the yeast into 30 ml (2 tbsp) of the warm water until smooth and well blended. Leave in a warm place for 15–20 minutes until frothy.

Mix the flour and salt together and gradually add the yeast mixture, the remaining water, the malt extract and the oil. Mix with a fork to form a firm dough that leaves the bowl clean.

Turn on to a floured board and knead for 5–10 minutes until elastic and smooth. Wash, dry and lightly oil the bowl. Replace the dough in the bowl, cover with a damp cloth and leave in a warm place for 1½–2 hours, until doubled in size.

Oil a baking tray. Turn the dough out on to a lightly floured board and knead for 2–3 minutes. Shape into a round and place on the prepared tray. Cover with cling film and leave in a warm place for 30 minutes, until doubled in size. Meanwhile, heat the oven to 425°F (220°C/Gas 7).

Bake the loaf for 35–40 minutes. Remove from the oven and test by tapping the bottom of the loaf lightly with your knuckles. If it sounds hollow, it is cooked. If not, return it to the oven and bake for a further 5 minutes. Remove from the oven and transfer to a wire rack to cool.

INGREDIENTS

10 ml (2 tsp) margarine, to grease tin and baking tray

350 g (12 oz) plain flour, sifted

Good pinch of salt

½ tsp bicarbonate of soda

5 ml (1 tsp) baking powder

5 ml (1 tsp) ground mixed spice

250 g (9 oz) sultanas or raisins, or a mixture of both

45 ml (3 tbsp) demerara sugar

275 ml (½ pt) malt extract

2 medium eggs, beaten

150 ml (¼ pt) milk

◆ MALT LOAF ◆

It is important to cover this loaf while it is cooking as it tends to brown on the top. It should be stored for 2–3 days before being eaten. Slice and spread with butter or cream cheese and preserves.

◆ **Preparation** 20 minutes ◆ **Cooking** 1½–1¾ hours ◆ **Makes** 18 cm (7 in) square loaf ◆

METHOD

Heat the oven to 300°F (150°C/Gas 2). Grease and line an 18 cm (7 in) square tin, with a depth of 6 cm (2½ in). Grease the base of a baking tray large enough to cover the tin.

Mix together the flour, salt, soda, baking powder and spice in a bowl. Stir in the dried fruit.

In a saucepan, slowly heat the sugar and malt extract. Do not boil. Pour the malt mixture into the dry ingredients and beat well with a wooden spoon. Beat the eggs and gradually add with the milk to the mixture, beating hard until the mixture is well blended.

Turn into the prepared tin. Cover with the baking tray, greased side down. Place an ovenproof weight on top and bake for 1½–1¾ hours. To test when the loaf is cooked, remove the weight and the baking tray and insert a skewer to see if it comes out clean.

Remove from the oven and turn out on to a wire rack to cool. When cold, wrap in foil and store for 2–3 days before serving.

♦ MARMALADE TEA LOAF ♦

This tea bread has the slightly bitter taste of marmalade, making it a good choice for those who do not like the sweetness of some fruit loaves. It is best stored for 3–4 days before eating.

♦ **Preparation** 15 minutes ♦ **Cooking** 1¼–1½ hours ♦ **Makes** 900 g (2 lb) loaf ♦

METHOD

Heat the oven to 350°F (180°C/Gas 4) and grease and line a 900 g (2 lb) loaf tin.

Mix the flour, salt and nutmeg together in a bowl and rub or cut in the fat until the mixture resembles fine breadcrumbs. Stir in the sugar. Add the egg, milk, orange rind and 60 ml (4 tbsp) of the marmalade, and beat thoroughly for 3–4 minutes until well blended.

Turn into the prepared tin and bake for 1¼–1½ hours, until a skewer comes out clean. Remove from the oven and turn out on to a wire rack. While still hot, spread the rest of the marmalade over the top. Leave to cool and then wrap in foil and store for 3–4 days before eating.

INGREDIENTS

225 g (8 oz) self-raising flour, sifted
Pinch of salt
7.5 ml (1½ tsp) ground nutmeg
100 g (4 oz) butter or margarine, softened, plus 5 ml (1 tsp) to grease tin
100 g (4 oz) demerara or soft brown sugar
1 large egg, beaten
60 ml (4 tbsp) milk
Grated rind of 1 orange
100 g (4 oz) chunky or ginger marmalade

♦ OAT BREAD ♦

This bread is excellent with cheese, cold meat and pâtés.

♦ **Preparation** 3¼–3½ hours ♦ **Cooking** 40–45 minutes ♦ **Makes** 2 × 900 g (2 lb) loaves ♦

METHOD

Cream the yeast and the white sugar together until smooth. Add the water and blend thoroughly. Leave the bowl in a warm place for 15–20 minutes until frothy.

In a saucepan, slowly heat the milk, brown sugar and butter, stirring gently until the sugar is dissolved. Remove from the heat and leave to cool.

Heat the oven to 275°F (140°C/Gas 1). Place the flour, salt and oats in an ovenproof bowl and warm in the oven for a few minutes. Switch off the oven. Make a well in the middle of the flour and pour in the yeast and the milk mixtures. Using a fork, gradually mix the flour and oats into the liquid to form a dough. The dough should be stiff, and should

INGREDIENTS

15 g (½ oz) fresh yeast
½ tsp caster sugar
45 ml (3 tbsp) warm water
225 ml (8 fl oz) milk
50 g (2 oz) soft brown sugar
50 g (2 oz) butter, plus 25 g (1 oz) to glaze bread
675 g (1½ lb) plain flour, sifted, plus 50–75 g (2–3 oz) to flour board
5 ml (1 tsp) salt
350 g (12 oz) rolled oats
10 ml (2 tsp) oil, to grease tins

Pictured opposite page 32

Continued overleaf

leave the bowl clean. If it is too wet, add more flour; if too dry, add a little more warm milk.

Turn on to a floured board and knead for about 10 minutes until smooth and elastic. Wash, dry and lightly grease the bowl. Return the dough to the bowl, cover with a damp cloth and leave in a warm place for 1¾–2 hours until doubled in size.

Oil 2 × 900 g (2 lb) loaf tins. Melt the extra 25 g (1 oz) butter for the glaze. Turn the dough on to the floured board and knead again for 4–5 minutes.

Divide the dough into 2 equal portions and shape to fit the tins. Place the loaves in the prepared tins and brush all over with the melted butter. Cover with a damp cloth and leave in a warm place for 1 hour until the dough has almost doubled in size and risen to the tops of the tins. Meanwhile, heat the oven to 425°F (220°C/Gas 7).

Bake the loaves for 15 minutes. Then, reduce the heat to 375°F (190°C/Gas 5) and bake for a further 25 minutes. Remove from the oven and tip the loaves out. Tap the bottoms gently with your knuckles. If they sound hollow, they are cooked. If not, lower the oven to 325°F (170°C/Gas 3), replace the loaves upside-down in the tins and bake for a further 5 minutes. Remove from the oven and transfer to a wire rack to cool.

INGREDIENTS

10 ml (2 tsp) oil, to grease tins
20 g (¾ oz) fresh yeast
¾ tsp caster sugar
700 ml (1¼ pt) warm water,
    plus 15–30 ml (1–2 tbsp)
    extra if necessary
900 g (2 lb) strong plain flour,
    sifted, plus 50–75 g
    (2–3 oz) to flour board
10 ml (2 tsp) salt

Continued on page 33

◆ WHITE BREAD ◆

This bread is soft and light, but with a good texture and flavour. For a tasty variation, make raisin bread by adding 5 ml (1 tsp) ground mixed spice to the flour and salt and adding 225 g (8 oz) raisins before kneading the dough for the second time. Make sure the fruit is evenly distributed throughout the dough.

◆ **Preparation** 2½–3 hours ◆ **Cooking** 1 hour ◆ **Makes** 2 × 900 g (2 lb) loaves ◆

METHOD

Oil 2 × 900 g (2 lb) loaf tins and leave in a warm place until needed.

Cream the yeast and the sugar together well. Pour the warm water on to the yeast mixture and blend thoroughly.

Sift the flour and salt into a bowl and make a well in the middle of the flour. Pour in the yeast liquid and sprinkle a little flour over the top of the liquid. Do not mix. Stand in a warm place for about 20 minutes.

After standing, mix with a fork to form an elastic dough, adding a little more warm water if necessary. Knead well until the dough comes

---

Breads & tea breads Clockwise from left: Oat bread (see page 31); Bara brith (see page 27); Fig loaf (see page 29).

cleanly away from the sides of the bowl. Place the dough in a warm place, cover with a damp cloth and leave to rise for about $1\frac{1}{2}$–2 hours, until doubled in size.

Turn on to a floured board and knead lightly again until there are only small holes in the dough. Divide the dough into 2 equal portions and shape to fit the warmed tins. Place the loaves in the tins, cover with a damp cloth and leave in a warm place for another 30–40 minutes, until the dough has almost doubled in size and risen to the tops of the tins. Meanwhile, heat the oven to 425°F (220°C/Gas 7).

Bake the loaves for 1 hour. Remove from the oven and tip the loaves out. Tap the bottoms gently with your knuckles. If they sound hollow, they are cooked. If not, replace the loaves upside-down in the tins and bake for a further 5 minutes. Remove from the oven and leave to cool in the tins for 2–3 minutes before turning out the loaves on to a wire rack to cool completely.

♦ WHOLEWHEAT BREAD ♦

This nutritious, tasty bread can be made in a loaf shape or as little rolls. Both methods are given below.

♦ **Preparation** 2 hours ♦ **Cooking** 40–50 minutes ♦ **Makes** 2 × 900 g (2 lb) loaves ♦

METHOD

Cream the honey and yeast together with a metal spoon until smooth and well blended. Add 150 ml ($\frac{1}{4}$ pt) of the warm water and mix well. Cover with a clean cloth and leave in a warm place for 10–15 minutes until frothy. Then beat the oil into the mixture.

Sift the flour and salt into a bowl and make a well in the middle. Pour the yeast and oil mixture into the well and, using a fork, gradually mix the flour into the liquid. Mix in enough of the remaining warm water to form a stiff dough.

Turn the dough on to a well floured board and knead with well floured hands for about 10 minutes, until it feels smooth and elastic. Add more flour if necessary. Replace the dough in the bowl, cover with a damp cloth and leave in a warm place for about 1 hour until it has doubled in size.

Oil 2 × 900 g (2 lb) loaf tins. Turn the dough on to a floured board and knead again for 5 minutes. Divide into 2 equal portions and shape to fit the prepared tins. Place in the tins and leave in a warm place for a further 30 minutes until the dough has almost doubled in size and risen to the tops of the tins. Meanwhile, heat the oven to 400°F (200°C/Gas 6).

INGREDIENTS

5 ml (1 tsp) honey

20 g ($\frac{3}{4}$ oz) fresh yeast

About 425 ml ($\frac{3}{4}$ pt) warm water

15 ml (1 tbsp) vegetable oil, plus 10 ml (2 tsp) to grease tins

550 g ($1\frac{1}{4}$ lb) plain wholewheat flour, sifted, plus 50–75 g (2–3 oz) to flour board

5 ml (1 tsp) salt

Continued overleaf

Sandwiches Smoked salmon (see page 41); Cucumber (see page 40).

Bake the loaves for 10 minutes, then turn down the heat to 350°F (180°C/Gas 4) and bake for a further 30–40 minutes. The loaves are cooked if they sound hollow when tapped lightly on the bottoms. Remove from the oven and leave to cool in the tins for 2–3 minutes before turning out on to a wire rack to cool completely.

ROLLS

To make wholewheat rolls, make the dough exactly as above, but instead of shaping it to fit the loaf tins, divide it into small balls of the size and number required. Shape and place them, spaced well apart, on greased baking trays. Cover with cling film and leave in a warm place for 20 minutes until the dough has doubled in size. Meanwhile, heat the oven to 400°F (200°C/Gas 6).

Bake the rolls for 20–25 minutes until puffed up and golden brown on top. Remove from the oven and transfer to a wire rack to cool.

♦ YOGHURT RYE BREAD ♦

The yogurt gives this bread a subtle moistness, and the rye flour a distinctive taste.

♦ **Preparation** 2½–3 hours ♦ **Cooking** 40–50 minutes ♦ **Makes** 900 g (2 lb) loaf ♦

INGREDIENTS

10 ml (2 tsp) honey
50 g (2 oz) fresh yeast
150 ml (¼ pt) warm water
400 g (14 oz) plain
   wholewheat flour, sifted,
   plus 50–75 g (2–3 oz) to
   flour board
100 g (4 oz) rye flour
10 ml (2 tsp) sea salt
150 ml (¼ pt) natural yogurt
30 ml (2 tsp) single cream
5 ml (1 tsp) oil, to grease tin

METHOD

Cream the honey and yeast together until smooth and well blended. Add the warm water and blend thoroughly. Leave in a warm place for 15–20 minutes until frothy.

Mix together the flours and salt in a bowl. Gradually stir in the yeast mixture, the yogurt and the cream, mixing with a fork to form a stiff, pliable dough.

Turn the dough on to a floured board and knead for 10–15 minutes. Wash, dry and lightly grease the bowl. Replace the dough in the bowl, cover with a damp cloth and leave in a warm place for 1½–2 hours, until doubled in size.

Oil a 900 g (2 lb) loaf tin and stand in a warm place until needed. Knead the dough again on a floured board for 5 minutes and then shape to fit the warmed tin. Place the loaf in the tin and leave in a warm place for 30–40 minutes until the dough has almost doubled in size and risen to the top of the tin. Meanwhile, heat the oven to 350°F (180°C/Gas 4).

Bake the loaf for 40–45 minutes. Remove from the oven, turn the loaf out and tap the bottom lightly with your knuckles. If it sounds hollow, it is cooked. If not, replace the loaf upside-down in the tin and bake for a further 5 minutes. Remove from the oven and turn out to cool on a wire rack.

SANDWICHES

Sandwiches are perfect for tea time, as they can be served at a variety of occasions. They make attractive, tasty additions to an afternoon tea, and can be as simple or elegant as required, depending on the filling used.

The best sandwiches should be a fine blending of textures and tastes, the type of bread playing as important a part as the filling. In the recipes which follow, the most suitable bread is suggested for each. Recipes for many breads are given in the previous chapter.

Butter should be spread on the sandwiches to add extra flavour and to prevent the fillings from soaking into the bread. Unsalted, slightly salted or salted butter is recommended in each recipe, or one of the special flavoured butters included in this chapter. Margarine should never, in my opinion, be used as it spoils the flavour.

Instructions have been given as to whether the crusts should be left on or off. Sandwiches can be cut into triangles, fingers or squares, as required. Try a variety of shapes to add interest to a platter of different sandwiches. Garnishes provide a final touch of elegance, and suggested trimmings are given for each sandwich.

BUTTERS

♦ ANCHOVY BUTTER ♦

This butter is especially good with egg and fish fillings.

♦ **Preparation** 10 minutes ♦ **Makes** Enough for 10 sandwiches ♦

INGREDIENTS
3 anchovies, washed and boned
100 g (4 oz) slightly salted or unsalted butter, softened
Shake of cayenne pepper

METHOD
Pound the anchovies with a pestle and mortar until pasty, or rub through a metal sieve.

Beat the butter thoroughly until light and fluffy. Mix with the anchovy paste, add a light shake of cayenne and beat well to blend.

INGREDIENTS
100 g (4 oz) slightly salted or
  unsalted butter, softened
10 ml (2 tsp) medium curry
  powder
½ tsp freshly squeezed lemon
  juice

♦ CURRY BUTTER ♦

Curry butter is excellent with meats, particularly chicken and ham.

♦ **Preparation** 5 minutes ♦ **Makes** Enough for 10 sandwiches ♦

METHOD

Beat the butter thoroughly until light and fluffy. Stir in the curry
powder and lemon juice and beat well to blend.

INGREDIENTS
100 g (4 oz) salted or slightly
  salted butter, softened
30 ml (2 tbsp) finely chopped
  fresh parsley
15 ml (1 tbsp) freshly
  squeezed lemon juice
Few drops of anchovy essence
Salt and freshly ground black
  pepper

♦ GREEN BUTTER ♦

The mild parsley flavour of this butter is good with most fillings,
particularly ham, sardine and pâté.

♦ **Preparation** 10 minutes ♦ **Makes** Enough for 10 sandwiches ♦

METHOD

Beat the butter thoroughly until light and fluffy. Add all the other
ingredients and beat well to blend.

INGREDIENTS
100 g (4 oz) salted or slightly
  salted butter, softened
1 sprig each of fresh parsley,
  chervil and tarragon,
  chopped very finely
1 small shallot, chopped very
  finely
Pinch of ground mace or
  nutmeg
Freshly ground black pepper

♦ HERB BUTTER ♦

Herb butter has a flavour which combines well with beef, ham
and tongue.

♦ **Preparation** 10 minutes ♦ **Makes** Enough for 10 sandwiches ♦

METHOD

Beat the butter thoroughly until light and fluffy. Add all the other
ingredients and beat well to blend.

INGREDIENTS
100 g (4 oz) salted or slightly
  salted butter, softened
5 ml (1 tsp) whole-grain
  mustard
Salt, to taste
Freshly ground black pepper

♦ MUSTARD BUTTER ♦

This is excellent with eggs, ham, pâté, pork and beef.

♦ **Preparation** 10 minutes ♦ **Makes** Enough for 10 sandwiches ♦

METHOD

Beat the butter thoroughly until light and fluffy. Add all the other
ingredients and beat well to blend.

FILLED SANDWICHES

Note: *'Makes 1 sandwich' refers to a double slice of bread, regardless of the number of cut squares, fingers, etc.*

♦ ANCHOVY & EGG ♦

This filling is deliciously creamy, with the strong salty flavour of anchovies. Decorate the sandwiches with small bunches of watercress.

♦ **Preparation** 10 minutes ♦ **Makes** 3–4 sandwiches ♦

METHOD
Pound together with a pestle and mortar or in a liquidizer the anchovies, egg yolks, cheese, cayenne and cream, using enough of the cream to make a smooth blend.

Spread the bread with the butter. Spread half the slices with the anchovy and egg mixture, not too thickly as it is quite rich and strong.

Press the other slices of bread on top. Trim off the crusts and cut into fingers or triangles.

INGREDIENTS
20 anchovies, washed and boned
6 medium hard-boiled egg yolks
50 g (2 oz) grated Parmesan or Cheddar cheese
Pinch of cayenne pepper
30–45 ml (2–3 tbsp) double cream
6–8 slices of bread
25–50 g (1–2 oz) unsalted butter

♦ ASPARAGUS & HAM ♦

For this combination the asparagus spears may be canned but they need to be firm and very well drained, otherwise the bread becomes extremely soggy. The ham should be home-cured if possible. Decorate with watercress sprigs or cucumber twists.

♦ **Preparation** 3 minutes ♦ **Makes** 3–4 sandwiches ♦

METHOD
Spread the bread generously with the mustard butter or herb butter, to help stop the juices from the asparagus seeping through.

Place the ham over half the slices of bread and lay over the asparagus. Press the other slices on top, leave the crusts on and cut into little squares or triangles.

INGREDIENTS
6–8 slices of bread
25–50 g (1–2 oz) herb butter or mustard butter (see opposite)
175–225 g (7–8 oz) home-cured ham, sliced
15–16 cooked slim asparagus spears, well drained if canned

Pictured opposite page 17

INGREDIENTS

6–8 slices of bread
25–50 g (1–2 oz) mustard
  butter (see page 36)
15 ml (1 tbsp) mayonnaise
225 g (8 oz) cold beef, sliced
3 medium hard-boiled eggs,
  sliced

♦ BEEF MAYONNAISE ♦

This sandwich is also delicious made with hot meat straight from the oven, with the juices from the meat spread on to the bread. Decorate with radish slices or watercress sprigs.

♦ **Preparation** 8–10 minutes ♦ **Makes** 3–4 sandwiches ♦

METHOD

Spread the bread with the mustard butter. Spread half the slices thinly with the mayonnaise. Lay slices of beef on top of the mayonnaise and arrange the slices of egg on top.

Press the other slices of bread on top. Leave the crusts on and cut into squares or triangles.

INGREDIENTS

6–8 slices of bread
25–50 g (1–2 oz) butter,
  mayonnaise or mustard
  butter (see page 36)
200 g (7 oz) blue cheese
15–20 sprigs of watercress,
  broken into smaller sprigs

BLUE CHEESE & ♦ WATERCRESS ♦

Use a creamy blue cheese such as Dolcelatte or a creamy Stilton. Decorate with watercress, cucumber twists or slices of radish.

♦ **Preparation** 5 minutes ♦ **Makes** 3–4 sandwiches ♦

METHOD

Spread the bread evenly with the butter, a thin layer of mayonnaise, or mustard butter. Cover half the slices of bread generously with the cheese and then lay the sprigs of watercress on top. Press the other slices of bread on top. Trim off the crusts and cut into squares or triangles.

INGREDIENTS

⅔ cucumber, peeled and sliced
  thinly
Salt and freshly ground black
  pepper
5 ml (1 tsp) freshly squeezed
  lemon juice
6–8 slices of bread
25–50 g (1–2 oz) slightly
  salted or unsalted butter
225 g (8 oz) mature Cheddar
  cheese, grated
15 ml (1 tbsp) chopped fresh
  chives (optional)

Pictured opposite page 129

♦ CHEESE & CUCUMBER ♦

For a really tasty sandwich, use a strongly flavoured Cheddar.

♦ **Preparation** 6–8 minutes ♦ **Makes** 3–4 sandwiches ♦

METHOD

Reserve 12 slices of cucumber for decoration. Place the remaining cucumber slices in a container and add the salt, pepper and lemon juice. Turn the cucumber in the seasoning so that each slice is coated.

Spread the bread with the butter. Pile the grated cheese on to half the bread. Cover with slices of the prepared cucumber and, if liked, sprinkle on a few freshly chopped chives.

Press the other slices of bread on top, trim off the crusts and cut into squares or triangles. Decorate with the reserved cucumber slices.

◆ CHICKEN MAYONNAISE ◆

This filling is very good with wholewheat rolls or soft white buns.
Decorate with cress or sprigs of watercress.

◆ **Preparation** 5 minutes ◆ **Makes** 3–4 rolls ◆

METHOD

Mix the chopped chicken with the mayonnaise, and season with salt and pepper. Add the chives if liked.

Split each roll across the middle and scoop out some of the centre from the bottom half of each roll to make a hollow. Spread each shell with the butter or green butter.

Spread a little of the chicken mixture into each hollowed bottom and place a generous portion of mustard and cress on top. Spread over the remaining chicken mixture and then replace the tops of the rolls.

INGREDIENTS

225 g (8 oz) cooked chicken, chopped
25 ml (1½ tbsp) mayonnaise
Salt and freshly ground black pepper
15 ml (1 tbsp) chopped fresh chives (optional)
6–8 rolls
25–50 g (1–2 oz) slightly salted butter or green butter (see page 36)
3 punnets of mustard and cress

COTTAGE CHEESE, ◆ HAM & PEACH ◆

Decorate with slices of peach, radish slices or cucumber twists.

◆ **Preparation** 5 minutes ◆ **Makes** 3–4 sandwiches ◆

METHOD

Chop the peaches into chunks and mix into the cottage cheese. Season with salt and black pepper to taste.

Spread the bread with the mustard butter. Lay the slices of ham over half the slices of bread and pile on the cheese and peach mixture.

Press the other slices of bread on top. Trim off the crusts and cut carefully into squares or triangles.

INGREDIENTS

2–3 fresh peaches, skinned, or 5–6 canned peach halves
225 g (8 oz) carton of cottage cheese
Salt and freshly ground black pepper
6–8 slices of bread
25–50 g (1–2 oz) mustard butter (see page 36)
4 thick slices of ham

◆ CREAM CHEESE & DATE ◆

This is a delicious combination that tastes best on wholewheat bread.
Decorate with date halves or slices of date.

◆ **Preparation** 5 minutes ◆ **Makes** 3–4 sandwiches ◆

METHOD

Spread the bread with the butter. Cover half the slices generously with cream cheese. Lay over the pieces of chopped date and sprinkle with a little cinnamon if liked.

Press the other slices of bread on top. Trim off the crusts and cut into squares or triangles.

INGREDIENTS

6–8 slices of bread
25–50 g (1–2 oz) slightly salted butter
175 g (6 oz) cream cheese, softened
75 g (3 oz) plump dried dates, stoned and chopped finely
Ground cinnamon (optional)

INGREDIENTS

½ cucumber, peeled and sliced
   thinly
Salt and freshly ground black
   pepper
5 ml (1 tsp) freshly squeezed
   lemon juice
6–8 slices of bread
25–50 g (1–2 oz) slightly
   salted butter or green
   butter (see page 36)

Pictured opposite pages 17, 33

♦ CUCUMBER ♦

*It is best to use soft white bread for this sandwich as the stronger flavour
and texture of wholewheat bread can overwhelm the subtle flavour of
the cucumber.*

♦ **Preparation** 10 minutes ♦ **Makes** 3–4 sandwiches ♦

METHOD

Reserve 12 slices of cucumber for decoration. Place the remaining
cucumber slices in a container and add the salt, pepper and lemon juice.
Turn the cucumber in the seasoning so that each slice is coated.

Spread the bread evenly with the butter or green butter. Cover half
the slices generously with the prepared cucumber.

Press the other slices on top. Trim off the crusts and cut into triangles.
To decorate, use the reserved slices of cucumber to make twists or lay 3
half-slices overlapping each other in a fan-like arrangement.

INGREDIENTS

3 medium eggs
30 ml (2 tbsp) mayonnaise
Salt and freshly ground black
   pepper
6–8 slices of bread
25–50 g (1–2 oz) slightly
   salted butter, or one of
   the flavoured butters
   suggested
2 punnets of mustard and
   cress

EGG MAYONNAISE &
♦ CRESS ♦

*This is probably one of the most delicious sandwich fillings. If you want
a slightly more unusual flavour, add chopped chives, mint or parsley, or
add a sprinkle of curry powder. Alternatively, spread the bread with
anchovy butter, curry butter or herb butter (see pages 35 and 36).
Wholewheat bread is very good for this sandwich. Decorate with neat
bunches of cress.*

♦ **Preparation** 15 minutes ♦ **Makes** 3–4 sandwiches ♦

METHOD

Boil the eggs for 6–8 minutes. Drain immediately and run under cold
water to stop them from cooking further. Shell the eggs and mash with
a strong fork until the whites are finely chopped; you can do this with
the medium grater attachment on a food processor, but the whites of
the eggs may need an extra mash with a fork afterwards to chop them
up evenly.

Add the mayonnaise, salt and pepper to the eggs and blend well so
that the egg is distributed evenly through the mayonnaise.

Spread the bread with the butter or flavoured butter. Spread the egg
mayonnaise generously over half the slices of bread and scatter over the
cress carefully and evenly.

Press the other slices of bread on top. Trim off the crusts and cut into
triangles or squares.

♦ PRINCESS ♦

This is a tasty combination of chicken, ham, cheese and eggs, and is excellent with curry butter or mustard butter. Decorate with cucumber slices or cress.

♦ **Preparation** 5–10 minutes ♦ **Makes** 3–4 sandwiches ♦

METHOD

Mix together the oil, vinegar, salt and pepper, and blend with the chopped meats, cheese and egg yolks. Make sure that the mixture is well blended.

Spread the bread generously with the curry butter or mustard butter. Cover half the slices with the meat mixture.

Press the other slices of bread on top. Trim off the crusts and cut into squares or triangles.

INGREDIENTS

10 ml (2 tsp) sunflower oil
Dash of tarragon or cider vinegar
Salt and freshly ground black pepper
150 g (5 oz) cooked chicken, chopped into small pieces
75 g (3 oz) cooked ham or tongue, chopped
15 g (½ oz) mature Cheddar cheese, grated
2 hard-boiled egg yolks
6–8 slices of bread
25–50 g (1–2 oz) curry or mustard butter (see page 36)

♦ SARDINE & TOMATO ♦

If possible, use freshly picked tomatoes, and nutty wholewheat bread. Decorate with tomato or cucumber slices.

♦ **Preparation** 5 minutes ♦ **Makes** 3–4 sandwiches ♦

METHOD

Drain the sardines, remove the bones and mash with the lemon juice.

Spread the bread with the slightly salted butter or herb butter. Cover half the slices of bread with the sardine mixture. Lay over the slices of tomato and season well with salt and pepper.

Press the other slices of bread on top. Cut carefully into squares or triangles, leaving the crusts on to stop the tomato from sliding out.

INGREDIENTS

2 × 124 g (4.37 oz) cans of sardines in oil
Few drops of freshly squeezed lemon juice
6–8 slices of bread
25–50 g (1–2 oz) slightly salted butter or herb butter (see page 36)
4–5 firm tomatoes, sliced thinly
Salt and black pepper

Pictured opposite page 129

♦ SMOKED SALMON ♦

This is the most self-indulgent, luxurious of sandwiches. Use wholewheat bread if possible, and decorate with neat twists or wedges of lemon.

♦ **Preparation** 5 minutes ♦ **Makes** 3–4 sandwiches ♦

METHOD

Spread the bread with the butter. Lay the slices of salmon over half the slices of bread. If liked, add a thin layer of cream cheese. Sprinkle over the lemon juice and add a generous grinding of black pepper.

Press the other slices of bread on top, trim off the crusts and cut into little triangles.

INGREDIENTS

6–8 slices of bread
25–50 g (1–2 oz) slightly salted or unsalted butter
275–300 g (10–11 oz) sliced smoked salmon
30–45 ml (3–4 tbsp) cream cheese (optional)
5 ml (1 tsp) freshly squeezed lemon juice
Freshly ground black pepper

Pictured opposite page 33

INGREDIENTS

1 cucumber, peeled and sliced
thinly
Salt and freshly ground black
pepper
5 ml (1 tsp) freshly squeezed
lemon juice
198 g (7 oz) can of red salmon
5 ml (1 tsp) freshly squeezed
lemon juice or wine
vinegar
6–8 slices of bread
25–50 g (1–2 oz) slightly
salted or unsalted butter

TINNED SALMON & ◆ CUCUMBER ◆

Canned red salmon makes a rather special, juicy filling for wholewheat bread sandwiches and a little lemon juice or wine vinegar enhances the flavour. Decorate with cucumber twists.

◆ **Preparation** 12–15 minutes ◆ **Makes** 3–4 sandwiches ◆

METHOD

Place the cucumber slices in a container and add the salt, pepper and first quantity of lemon juice. Turn the cucumber in the seasoning so that each slice is coated.

Drain the fish and remove any skin and bone. Mash the flesh and blend with the second quantity of lemon juice or vinegar, and add salt and pepper to taste.

Spread the bread evenly and quite thickly with the butter. Spread a generous layer of salmon over half the slices of bread. Lay slices of the prepared cucumber over the salmon.

Press the other slices of bread on top. Trim off the crusts and cut into neat squares or triangles.

INGREDIENTS

198 g (7 oz) can of tuna in oil
Dash of lemon juice or cider
vinegar
12–15 fresh mint leaves,
chopped finely
Salt and freshly ground black
pepper
6–8 slices of bread
25–50 g (1–2 oz) slightly
salted or unsalted butter
$\frac{1}{4}$ cucumber, sliced thinly
(optional)

◆ TUNA & MINT ◆

Fresh mint gives a wonderfully fresh taste to this sandwich. It is best to make the filling about 1 hour before using, to give the flavours time to blend. Use wholewheat bread and slightly salted or unsalted butter. Decorate with fresh mint or cucumber twists.

◆ **Preparation** 3–4 minutes, plus up to 1 hour to chill ◆ **Makes** 3–4 sandwiches ◆

METHOD

Drain the tuna and mash with a fork. Add the lemon juice or vinegar, the mint, and salt and pepper to taste, and blend together well. Leave to chill in the refrigerator, for up to 1 hour if possible.

Spread the bread generously with the butter. Pile the tuna mixture on to half the slices of bread and place over a few slices of cucumber if liked.

Press the other slices of bread on top. Trim off the crusts and cut into squares or triangles.

◆ TURKEY & CRANBERRY ◆

This is a very pretty sandwich and is good with white bread. Use meat from the breast of the turkey if possible, and a cranberry jelly that is fairly firm. Decorate with mustard and cress for a beautiful contrast of green, pink and white.

◆ **Preparation** 3 minutes ◆ **Makes** 3–4 sandwiches ◆

METHOD

Spread the bread evenly with the butter.

Cover half the slices of bread with the cranberry jelly or sauce, keeping it away from the edges of the bread. Lay the slices of turkey over the cranberry jelly.

Press the other slices of bread on top. Trim off the crusts and cut into squares or triangles.

INGREDIENTS

6–8 slices of bread
25–50 g (1–2 oz) slightly salted butter or mustard butter (see page 36)
15–20 ml (3–4 tsp) cranberry jelly or sauce
175 g (6 oz) turkey meat, sliced
Pinch of salt and pepper

WALNUTS, CHEDDAR CHEESE & ◆ LETTUCE ◆

For a satisfying contrast of flavours and textures the Cheddar should be strongly flavoured and the lettuce as crisp as possible. Use a nutty wholewheat bread. Decorate with cucumber twists or sprigs of watercress.

◆ **Preparation** 8–10 minutes ◆ **Makes** 3–4 sandwiches ◆

METHOD

Mix together the chopped walnuts and the cheese.

Spread the bread with the butter or mustard butter and cover half the slices with the walnut and cheese mixture. Carefully lay the shredded lettuce over the cheese and sprinkle with salt and pepper.

Press the other slices of bread on top. Trim off the crusts and cut into squares or triangles.

INGREDIENTS

100 g (4 oz) walnuts, chopped small
225 g (8 oz) mature Cheddar cheese, grated
6–8 slices of bread
25–50 g (1–2 oz) unsalted butter or mustard butter (see page 36)
A few crisp lettuce leaves, shredded
Salt and freshly ground black pepper

TEA TIME TRADITIONALS

Afternoon tea would not be complete without a selection of traditional items such as scones, muffins, crumpets, teacakes and hot buttered toast. Several of these are seasonal and so the choice of menu will depend on the time of year. In summer, Cornish splits, scones, strawberries and clotted cream are traditionally served. In winter, muffins, crumpets and other deliciously filling goodies are served hot and oozing with butter. In the days of open fires they were toasted in the drawing room over the heat of the embers on the end of a toasting fork.

INGREDIENTS
225 g (8 oz) plain flour, sifted, plus 50–75 g (2–3 oz) to flour board
15 g ($\frac{1}{2}$ oz) fresh yeast
5 ml (1 tsp) caster sugar
100 ml (4 fl oz) warm milk
$\frac{1}{2}$ tsp salt
15 g ($\frac{1}{2}$ oz) butter or lard, softened
1 medium egg, beaten
50 g (2 oz) melted butter or margarine, plus 5 ml (1 tsp) to grease tin
175 g (6 oz) mixed dried fruit (raisins, currants, sultanas and cherries)
25 g (1 oz) mixed candied peel
$\frac{1}{2}$ tsp ground mixed spice
50 g (2 oz) soft brown sugar
45 ml (3 tbsp) clear honey

Pictured opposite page 48

◆ CHELSEA BUNS ◆

These are deliciously sticky and filling. The dried fruit used may be a mixture of sultanas, raisins and currants, or just one of these.

◆ **Preparation** 2$\frac{1}{2}$–3 hours ◆ **Cooking** 30–35 minutes ◆ **Makes** 9 buns ◆

METHOD
Grease an 18 cm (7 in) square tin. Put 50 g (2 oz) of the flour into a bowl. Add the yeast, white sugar and milk and mix to a batter. Leave in a warm place for 15–20 minutes until frothy.

Put the remaining flour and the salt in a bowl and rub or cut in the fat until the mixture resembles fine breadcrumbs. Add this to the yeast mixture with the egg and mix to a soft dough that leaves the sides of the bowl clean.

Turn on to a floured board and knead for about 5 minutes until smooth and elastic. Place inside a large, well oiled plastic bag and leave in a warm place until doubled in size. This should take 1–1$\frac{1}{2}$ hours.

Turn out and knead again until smooth. Roll out to a rectangle about 30 × 24 cm (12 × 9$\frac{1}{2}$ in). Brush the entire surface with the melted butter or margarine. Mix together the fruit, peel, spice and brown sugar, and sprinkle all over the dough.

Starting from a long side, roll the dough up to form a long tube. Seal the ends with a little water. Cut crossways into 9 equal slices and place closely together in the prepared tin, cut side down. Cover with a plastic bag and leave in a warm place for about 30 minutes until doubled in size. Meanwhile, heat the oven to 375°F (190°C/Gas 5).

Remove the bag and bake the buns for 30–35 minutes until golden. Remove from the oven and turn out on to a wire rack so that the top side stays uppermost. While still warm, pull apart and brush with the honey. Leave to cool.

♦ CLOTTED CREAM ♦

Rich, thick clotted cream, traditionally from the West Country, is one of the most delicious accompaniments for cakes, pastries and desserts. It is usually served with warm scones and strawberry jam.

♦ **Preparation and cooking** About 20–30 minutes, plus 2–3 days to stand ♦
♦ **Makes** 225 g (8 oz) clotted cream ♦

METHOD

Leave the milk to stand covered for 24 hours in winter or for 12 hours in summer. Then, pour into a saucepan and slowly heat but do not allow to boil. The slower the milk is heated, the better. When small rings and undulations appear on the surface the scalding process is complete and the pan should be taken off the heat.

Cover and place the pan in a cool place (the refrigerator during summer) and leave until the following day. Skim the clotted cream off into a container and refrigerate. Do not freeze.

INGREDIENTS
4.5 ltr (8 pt) milk, with at least 56% cream content

♦ CORNISH SPLITS ♦

These buns are traditionally served in Cornwall, split open and spread with butter, jam, and clotted or whipped cream.

♦ **Preparation** 2–2½ hours ♦ **Cooking** 25 minutes ♦ **Makes** 20 splits ♦

METHOD

Grease 2 large baking trays.

Cream the yeast and sugar together until smooth. Add the water and blend thoroughly. Add 15 ml (1 tbsp) of the flour and mix carefully. Cover with a damp cloth and leave in a warm place for 15–20 minutes until frothy.

Heat the oven to 250°F (130°C/Gas ½). Put the lard, 100 g (4 oz) of the butter and the milk in an ovenproof bowl and place in the oven to

INGREDIENTS
25 g (1 oz) fresh yeast
½ tsp caster sugar
150 ml (¼ pt) warm water
675 g (1½ lb) strong plain flour, sifted, plus 50–75 g (2–3 oz) to flour board
25 g (1 oz) lard, softened
175 g (6 oz) butter, softened, plus 10 ml (2 tsp) to grease baking trays
75 ml (3 fl oz) milk
5 ml (1 tsp) salt

Pictured opposite page 48

Continued overleaf

warm. Put the remaining flour and salt in another ovenproof bowl and also place in the oven to warm.

Remove the bowls from the oven. Make a well in the middle of the flour and pour in the milk and fat mixture and the yeast batter. Using a fork, gradually mix the flour into the liquid; then, using floured hands, work the mixture to a smooth dough.

Turn on to a floured board and knead lightly for 2–3 minutes, until smooth and elastic. Place in a large clean, oiled bowl. Cover with a damp cloth and leave to rise in a warm place for 1–1½ hours, until doubled in size.

Turn out on to a floured board and knead lightly again until smooth and elastic. Divide into balls, about 2.5 cm (1 in) across, and press them flat to half their height. Place on the prepared trays and leave in a warm place for 30 minutes until doubled in size. Meanwhile, heat the oven to 350°F (180°C/Gas 4).

Bake the splits for 25 minutes, until light golden. Melt the remaining 50 g (2 oz) butter for the glaze. Remove the splits from the oven when cooked and transfer to a wire rack to cool. Brush the tops with the melted butter.

INGREDIENTS
350 g (12 oz) plain flour, sifted
½ tsp caster sugar
Pinch of salt
25 g (1 oz) fresh yeast
425 ml (¾ pt) warm milk
150 ml (¼ pt) warm water
2 medium eggs, beaten

Pictured opposite page 48

♦ CRUMPETS ♦

To serve crumpets, toast and spread liberally with butter.

♦ **Preparation** 1¾–2 hours ♦ **Cooking** About 1 hour ♦ **Makes** 20 crumpets ♦

METHOD

Mix the flour with the sugar and salt in a bowl. Dissolve the yeast in a little of the warm milk, and add to the flour with the remaining milk, the water and the beaten eggs. Beat hard to form a smooth batter and leave in a warm place for ½–¾ hour.

Beat again thoroughly and leave to stand in a warm place for a further 30 minutes. Repeat this process once more, beating and standing again for 30 minutes.

Place a griddle or heavy frying pan over a low to moderate heat and leave for a few minutes to reach a steady overall temperature. Place 4–5 crumpet rings on to the griddle or pan and then spoon a little batter, about 30 ml (2 tbsp), into each ring. Leave for about 6–8 minutes until the underside of each crumpet is light brown, and then turn the rings over carefully and brown the other side, again for about 6–8 minutes until light brown.

Transfer carefully to a wire rack to cool. Remove the rings and repeat the cooking procedure as above until all the batter is used up. Toast the crumpets before serving.

♦ DOUGHNUTS ♦

Traditionally, doughnuts are either made in rings, as here, or whole with jam centres (below). The basic method for each is the same.

♦ **Preparation** 2½ hours ♦ **Cooking** 15–20 minutes ♦ **Makes** 15 doughnuts ♦

INGREDIENTS

225 g (8 oz) plain flour, sifted, plus 45–60 ml (3–4 tbsp) to flour board
¼ tsp salt
20 g (¾ oz) lard, softened
25 g (1 oz) margarine, softened
15 g (½ oz) fresh yeast
25 g (1 oz) caster sugar, plus 15 ml (1 tbsp) to coat doughnuts
150 ml (¼ pt) warm milk
1 medium egg, beaten
15 ml (1 tbsp) ground cinnamon
Vegetable or corn oil, to deep-fry doughnuts

METHOD

Heat the oven to 275°F (130°C/Gas 1) and warm the flour and salt in an ovenproof bowl. Switch off the oven.

Rub or cut the lard and margarine into the flour until the mixture resembles breadcrumbs. Cream the yeast with 5 ml (1 tsp) of the sugar and blend thoroughly. Mix in the rest of the sugar and then the milk and the egg.

Make a well in the middle of the flour. Pour in the milk and yeast liquid and, using a fork, gradually mix the flour into the liquid to form a soft dough. Leave the dough in the bowl and stand in a warm place for about 1½–2 hours to rise.

Turn out on to a floured board and knead lightly for a few minutes. Roll out to a thickness of 1 cm (½ in). Cut into rings, using a 6 cm (2½ in) cutter dipped in flour, and then cut out the middles using a 4 cm (1½ in) cutter. Place the rings on a floured board and leave in a warm place to rise for 5–10 minutes.

Mix together the cinnamon and extra sugar in a shallow dish. Heat a saucepan half-full of oil until it is very hot and faintly smoking. Using a slotted spoon, drop 3–4 doughnuts carefully into the oil and cook for 4–5 minutes. Lift out, drain well on paper towels and then toss immediately in the cinnamon sugar. Keep warm. Repeat until all the doughnuts are cooked.

JAM DOUGHNUTS

Make the dough as above. When the dough has risen, knead lightly on a floured board and divide into 14–16 balls. With your thumb, make a deep indentation in each and place a teaspoonful of jam (strawberry or raspberry is traditional) into the hollow. Fold the dough back over the jam so that it is encased by dough. Seal well.

Place the balls on a floured board and leave in a warm place for 10–15 minutes to rise. Fry exactly as for ring doughnuts.

INGREDIENTS

15 g (½ oz) fresh yeast
15 ml (1 tbsp) caster sugar
275 ml (½ pt) warm water
450 g (1 lb) plain flour, sifted,
    plus 50–75 g (2–3 oz) to
    flour board
10 ml (2 tsp) salt
30 ml (2 tbsp) oil, to grease
    bowl and tin
400 g (14 oz) lard, softened
175 g (6 oz) granulated sugar
¼ tsp nutmeg, cinnamon or
    allspice
50 g (2 oz) sultanas or raisins
50 g (2 oz) sugar cubes,
    crushed

◆ LARDY CAKE ◆

Lardy cake is an enriched bread traditionally associated with Wiltshire and Gloucestershire. Lard, sugar and dried fruit is added to bread dough for a wonderfully soft, moist and spicy treat.

◆ **Preparation** 1½–2 hours ◆ **Cooking** 30 minutes ◆ **Makes** 9 pieces ◆

METHOD

Cream the yeast with the caster sugar and water. Mix the flour and salt together in a bowl and make a well in the middle. Pour in the yeast mixture and, using a fork, gradually mix to a soft dough.

Turn on to a floured board and knead for about 5 minutes until smooth and elastic. Wash, dry and lightly oil the bowl, replace the dough in it and cover with a damp cloth. Leave in a warm place for 1–1½ hours until doubled in size.

Heat the oven to 400°F (200°C/Gas 6) and oil a 20 cm (8 in) square tin. Turn the dough on to a floured board and knead again for 5 minutes. Roll out into a rectangle about 1 cm (½ in) thick. Dot the surface with a third of the lard and sprinkle with a third of the sugar. Fold the bottom third of the dough up and the top third down over it. Turn the dough so that the folded sides are on your left and right.

Roll out again to a rectangle. Dot the surface with another third of the lard and sprinkle with another third of the sugar. Repeat the folding, rolling, dotting and sprinkling once more. On the last dotting and sprinkling, also sprinkle over the spices, dried fruit and crushed cube sugar. Fold and roll out to a square the size of the prepared tin.

Place the dough in the tin and mark into 9 squares. Bake for 30 minutes until pale golden. Remove from the oven and turn out on to a wire rack to cool. When cool, break (do not cut) into pieces.

INGREDIENTS

10 ml (2 tsp) margarine, to
    grease baking trays
450 g (1 lb) plain flour, sifted
½ tsp salt
15 g (½ oz) fresh yeast
5 ml (1 tsp) caster sugar
275 ml (½ pt) warm milk

Continued on page 49

◆ MUFFINS ◆

The correct way to serve muffins is not to split them and toast both halves, which makes them tough, but to pull the muffin open to a depth of about 2.5 cm (1 in) and then toast the two halves, closed together, slowly and carefully so that the inside is warmed as well as the outside being browned. When toasted, split open and serve with plenty of butter.

◆ **Preparation** 1½–2 hours ◆ **Cooking** 15–16 minutes ◆ **Makes** 10–12 muffins ◆

Tea time traditionals Clockwise from left: Wholewheat scones (see page 52); Chelsea buns (see page 44); Cornish splits (see page 45); Scottish drop scones (see page 50); Crumpets (see page 46).

METHOD

Grease 2 large, heavy baking trays.

Mix the flour and salt together in a bowl. In a separate bowl, cream the yeast with the sugar until smooth and mix into the flour with a little of the warm milk. Add the rest of the milk and mix with a fork to form a stiff dough.

In the bowl, knead the dough well for 5–10 minutes. Leave the bowl in a warm place for about 1–1½ hours, covered, until doubled in size. Turn the dough on to a lightly floured board and knead again until smooth and elastic.

Roll the dough out to a thickness of about 1 cm (½ in). Cut out circles using a 7.5 cm (3 in) cutter dipped in flour. Place the circles on the prepared trays and leave in a warm place for 10–15 minutes until doubled in size. Meanwhile, heat the oven to 425°F (220°C/Gas 7).

Bake for about 7–8 minutes until slightly browned on top. Turn the muffins over carefully and cook for a further 7–8 minutes to brown the other side. Remove the muffins from the oven and transfer to a wire rack to cool.

◆ SCONES ◆

These should be served warm and are delicious halved and spread with jam and clotted or whipped cream.

◆ **Preparation** 10 minutes ◆ **Cooking** 12–15 minutes ◆ **Makes** 10–12 scones ◆

METHOD

Heat the oven to 450°F (230°C/Gas 8). Grease a baking tray and dredge with flour.

Mix together the flour and salt. Rub or cut in the butter as lightly as possible until the mixture resembles breadcrumbs. Stir in the sugar. Add the egg and bind the mixture together with a fork. Gradually add the milk to form a fairly stiff dough.

Turn the dough on to a floured board and gently roll out to a thickness of about 2½ cm (1 in). Cut out circles using a 6 cm (2½ in) cutter dipped in flour. Place the scones, almost touching, on the prepared tray and brush with beaten egg or milk to glaze.

Bake for 12–15 minutes until firm and light golden. Remove from the oven and slide the scones on to a wire rack. Cover immediately with a cloth to keep the steam in. This helps make the scones deliciously soft and moist.

INGREDIENTS

225 g (8 oz) self-raising flour, sifted, plus 45–60 ml (3–4 tbsp) to flour baking tray and board
Pinch of salt
50 g (2 oz) butter, softened, plus 5 ml (1 tsp) to grease baking tray
25 g (1 oz) caster sugar
1 medium egg, beaten
75 ml (3 fl oz) milk
Beaten egg or milk, to glaze scones

Pictured opposite page 17

Continued overleaf

Biscuits Clockwise from top: Coffee creams (see page 54); Cornish fairings (see page 54); Shrewsbury biscuits (see page 57).

VARIATIONS

Cheese scones: Make exactly as for scones, above, but leave out the sugar and add a pinch of dry mustard powder and 25 g (1 oz) of grated mature Cheddar cheese to the flour and butter mixture before you add the beaten egg.

Fruit scones: Make exactly as for scones, above, but add 50 g (2 oz) raisins or sultanas to the mixture before you add the egg.

Lemon scones: Make exactly as for scones, above, but add the finely grated rind of 1 lemon and replace 15 ml (1 tbsp) of the milk with lemon juice.

INGREDIENTS

225 g (8 oz) self-raising flour, sifted
Pinch of salt
5 ml (1 tsp) cream of tartar
½ tsp bicarbonate of soda
25 g (1 oz) caster sugar
1 large egg, beaten
225 ml (8 fl oz) warm milk
Oil or lard, to grease griddle

Pictured opposite page 48

◆ SCOTTISH DROP SCONES ◆

If you do not have a proper griddle for cooking these drop scones, use a heavy frying pan at a very low steady temperature. The scones are best served piping hot with honey, syrup or jam.

◆ **Preparation** 15 minutes ◆ **Cooking** 35–40 minutes ◆ **Makes** 18–20 scones ◆

METHOD

Mix together all the dry ingredients in a bowl. Make a well in the middle and pour the egg into it. Mix the egg gradually into the flour with a wooden spoon, working gently from the middle so that the egg picks up the flour. Very gradually add the milk and continue mixing until all the flour has been incorporated. Beat the mixture hard for 2–3 minutes.

Leave the batter to stand for 10 minutes. Meanwhile, warm the griddle and wipe over with oil or lard. Regulate the heat so that the griddle reaches an even all-over temperature. If it gets too hot the scones will burn before being cooked through.

Drop 4 separate tablespoonfuls of the batter on to the griddle. Leave to cook slowly until bubbles appear and break. After about 4 minutes, turn the scones over very carefully with a metal spatula. Leave for another 3–4 minutes until the undersides are golden. The scones should be a golden brown on both sides. Remove the scones from the griddle, grease it again and drop more spoonfuls of batter on to it.

Repeat until all the batter is used up. As the scones are cooked they should be placed inside a linen cloth to keep them warm and moist until all are ready to serve.

◆ TEACAKES ◆

These are lovely served warm from the oven, split open and spread with butter. Alternatively, they can be split in half, toasted and then buttered.

◆ **Preparation** 2–2¼ hours ◆ **Cooking** 10–15 minutes ◆ **Makes** 8–10 teacakes ◆

METHOD

Cream the yeast and sugar together until smooth. Gradually mix in the milk and blend thoroughly. Cover and leave in a warm place for 5–10 minutes until frothy.

Mix together the flour, salt and cinnamon in a bowl. Rub or cut in the butter lightly until the mixture resembles breadcrumbs. Make a well in the middle of the flour and pour the yeast mixture into it. Mix the flour into the liquid gradually with a fork to form a stiff dough. Place in a well greased bowl and cover with a damp cloth. Leave in a warm place for about 1–1½ hours until doubled in size.

Grease 2 baking trays. Turn the dough on to a floured board, scatter with the fruit and knead lightly until the fruit is evenly distributed throughout the dough.

Divide the dough into 8–10 balls, about 5 cm (2½ in) across. Pat into flat buns and place on the prepared trays. Leave for 30 minutes in a warm place to rise. Meanwhile, heat the oven to 400°F (200°C/Gas 6).

Brush the teacakes with the beaten egg and bake for 10–15 minutes until golden and firm. Remove from the oven and cool on a wire rack. For a sticky top, brush the teacakes with melted honey or syrup as soon as they are removed from the oven.

INGREDIENTS

15 g (½ oz) fresh yeast
75 g (3 oz) caster sugar
150 ml (¼ pt) warm milk
450 g (1 lb) plain flour, sifted, plus 50–75 g (2–3 oz) to flour board
Pinch of salt
¼ tsp ground cinnamon
50 g (2 oz) butter, softened, plus 10 ml (2 tsp) to grease baking trays
75 g (3 oz) mixed sultanas, raisins and candied peel
1 medium egg, beaten
Honey or syrup, melted (optional)

Pictured opposite page 129

◆ WELSH CAKES ◆

Welsh cakes were traditionally made with ewes' milk or cows' milk and baked on a 'bake-stone' or Dutch oven placed before the open fire. The Dutch oven was a semi-circular chamber, normally made from tin, with hooks for roasting meat and a perforated plate which served as a grid-iron. The cakes are best cooked on a griddle but a heavy frying pan will do. They are delicious eaten warm, spread with butter.

◆ **Preparation** 10 minutes ◆ **Cooking** 30–40 minutes ◆ **Makes** 8–10 cakes ◆

METHOD

Mix together the flour, sugar, salt and nutmeg in a bowl. Rub or cut in the fat until the mixture begins to stick together. Add the currants and egg and mix with a fork to form a stiff dough. If the dough is too dry, add a very little milk.

INGREDIENTS

225 g (8 oz) plain flour, sifted, plus 45–60 ml (3–4 tbsp) to flour board
75 g (3 oz) caster sugar
Pinch of salt
¾ tsp ground nutmeg
100 g (4 oz) margarine or butter, softened, plus 25 g (1 oz) to grease griddle
75 g (3 oz) currants
1 medium egg, beaten
15–30 ml (1–2 tbsp) warm milk (optional)

Continued overleaf

Roll the dough out on a floured board to a thickness of 2 cm (¾ in).
Cut into circles with a 7.5 cm (3 in) cutter dipped in flour.

Warm the griddle to a moderate heat and grease well. Leave for a few minutes to reach an even, all-over temperature, but do not let it get too hot or the cakes will burn before their insides are cooked.

Lay 4–5 cakes carefully on the griddle and leave to cook slowly (8–10 minutes for each side). When the undersides are browned, carefully turn over with a metal spatula and leave to brown on the other side. Repeat until all the cakes are cooked.

Remove the cakes carefully on to a wire rack as they are cooked and wrap in a linen cloth until all the cakes are ready to serve.

INGREDIENTS

50 g (2 oz) plain flour, sifted, plus 45–60 ml (3–4 tbsp) flour to flour baking tray and board
175 g (6 oz) plain wholewheat flour, sifted
Pinch of salt
15 ml (1 tbsp) baking powder
50 g (2 oz) butter or margarine, softened, plus 5 ml (1 tsp) to grease baking tray
25 g (1 oz) caster sugar
150 ml (¼ pt) milk or sour milk
Beaten egg or milk, to glaze scones

Pictured opposite page 48

◆ WHOLEWHEAT SCONES ◆

For wholewheat fruit scones, add 75 g (3 oz) raisins or sultanas to the mixture before adding the milk.

◆ **Preparation** 10 minutes ◆ **Cooking** 12–15 minutes ◆ **Makes** 10–12 scones ◆

METHOD

Heat the oven to 450°F (230°C/Gas 8). Grease a baking tray and dredge with flour.

Mix together the flours, salt and baking powder in a bowl. Rub or cut in the fat lightly until the mixture resembles breadcrumbs. Stir in the sugar. Gradually add the milk, using a fork, to form a stiff dough.

Roll the dough out lightly on a floured board to a thickness of about 2.5 cm (1 in). Cut out circles, using a 6 cm (2½ in) cutter dipped in flour. Place the scones on the prepared tray, almost touching, and brush with beaten egg or milk, to glaze.

Bake for 12–15 minutes until firm and lightly browned. Remove from the oven and transfer to a wire rack to cool. Cover immediately with a cloth to keep the steam in. This helps make the scones soft and deliciously moist.

BISCUITS

These recipes are for biscuits which are all delicious with morning coffee or with a late-night hot drink, as well as with afternoon tea.

It is a good idea to serve a selection of biscuits to provide variety of texture and flavour. To serve biscuits, arrange them on a round cake plate, in a pretty tin or on a rectangular sandwich tray.

When making biscuits it is always better to slightly undercook them than to overcook, as a minute too long in the oven will spoil the flavour and make them too dry and crunchy. After removing the biscuits from the oven, leave to cool for 2–3 minutes on the baking tray to allow them to set. If removed too soon they will collapse; if left for too long they will stick to the tray and may break when removed.

♦ ANZACS ♦

These biscuits are quite soft and chewy, with a lovely oat flavour.

♦ **Preparation** 10–15 minutes ♦ **Cooking** 15–20 minutes ♦ **Makes** 16–18 biscuits ♦

METHOD

Heat the oven to 350°F (180°C/Gas 4) and grease a baking tray.

Melt the fat and syrup gently in a fairly large saucepan. Remove the pan from the heat and mix in the oats, flour and sugar. Blend the mixture thoroughly.

Dissolve the soda in the boiling water. Stir into the mixture and mix well. With floured hands and a dessertspoon, scoop out spoonfuls of the mixture and roll them into balls. Place the balls on the prepared tray, spaced well apart.

Bake the biscuits for 15–20 minutes. Remove from the oven and leave to cool on the tray for 4–5 minutes before lifting carefully on to a wire rack to cool completely.

INGREDIENTS

100 g (4 oz) margarine or butter, plus 5 ml (1 tsp) to grease baking tray
15 ml (1 tbsp) syrup
225 g (8 oz) rolled oats
150 g (5 oz) self-raising flour, sifted, plus 45–60 ml (3–4 tbsp) to flour hands
100 g (4 oz) demerara sugar
5 ml (1 tsp) bicarbonate of soda
30 ml (2 tbsp) boiling water

INGREDIENTS

For the biscuits
50 g (2 oz) lard, softened, plus
   10 ml (2 tsp) to grease tins
50 g (2 oz) caster sugar
5 ml (1 tsp) syrup
1 medium egg, beaten
5 ml (1 tsp) instant coffee,
   dissolved in a few drops of
   boiling water
225 g (8 oz) self-raising flour,
   sifted
$\frac{1}{2}$ tsp salt

For the filling
50 g (2 oz) butter, softened
75 g (3 oz) icing sugar
5 ml (1 tsp) instant coffee,
   dissolved in a few drops of
   boiling water

Pictured opposite page 49

◆ COFFEE CREAMS ◆

These have a soft, crumbly texture. If desired, the coffee flavour can be made even stronger by increasing the quantity of instant coffee.

◆ **Preparation** 20 minutes ◆ **Cooking** 10–15 minutes ◆ **Makes** 15 biscuits ◆

METHOD

Heat the oven to 350°F (180°C/Gas 4) and grease 2 baking trays.

Cream the lard and sugar together until soft and fluffy. Add the syrup and beat the mixture well. Add the egg and the coffee and beat again, using a fork.

Mix in the flour and salt to form a stiff dough. Knead the dough for a few minutes in the bowl until smooth.

Divide the dough into 28–30 pieces and roll each between the palms of your hands to form a ball. Place the balls on the prepared trays, spaced well apart, and press each down with the prongs of a fork, making a pattern.

Bake the biscuits for 10–15 minutes until brown and firm. Remove from the oven and leave to cool on the tray for 2–3 minutes before lifting on to a wire rack to cool completely.

For the filling, mix all the ingredients together and beat until smooth. Use to sandwich the biscuits together.

INGREDIENTS

225 g (8 oz) plain flour, sifted,
   plus 45–60 ml (3–4 tbsp) to
   flour board
$\frac{1}{2}$ tsp ground mixed spice
$\frac{1}{2}$ tsp ground ginger
65 g (2$\frac{1}{2}$ oz) margarine,
   softened, plus 10 ml (2 tsp)
   to grease baking trays
25 g (1 oz) lard, softened
65 g (2$\frac{1}{2}$ oz) demerara sugar
10 ml (2 tsp) bicarbonate of
   soda
10 ml (2 tsp) cream of tartar
100 ml (4 fl oz) syrup,
   warmed by standing the
   tin in hot water

Pictured opposite page 49

◆ CORNISH FAIRINGS ◆

A traditional fairing was originally a gift bought at a fair. Later the term 'fairing' came to be used for any cakes or sweets sold at a fair. Here is one recipe.

◆ **Preparation** 10 minutes ◆ **Cooking** 15–20 minutes ◆ **Makes** 25 biscuits ◆

METHOD

Heat the oven to 350°F (180°C/Gas 4) and grease 2 large baking trays.

Mix together the flour, spice and ginger. Rub or cut in the fats until the mixture resembles breadcrumbs. Mix in the sugar. Blend the soda and the cream of tartar with the warmed syrup. Add this to the flour mixture and mix with a fork to form a soft paste.

Roll out the paste on a floured board to a thickness of 1 cm ($\frac{1}{2}$ in). Cut out squares or circles using a 5 cm (2 in) cutter. Place the biscuits carefully on the prepared trays, spaced well apart.

Bake the biscuits for 15–20 minutes until risen and golden brown. Remove from the oven and leave to cool on the trays for 2–3 minutes before transferring carefully to a wire rack to cool completely.

♦ JUMBLES ♦

These little 'S'-shaped biscuits have a sweet, bland flavour, popular with children.

♦ **Preparation** 20–25 minutes ♦ **Cooking** 15–20 minutes ♦ **Makes** 26–38 biscuits ♦

METHOD

Heat the oven to 350°F (180°C/Gas 4) and grease 2 large baking trays.

Cream the butter and sugar together until light and fluffy. Beat in the egg and almond essence. Fold in the flour and almonds with a metal spoon. Using floured hands, knead the mixture until it is a firm but pliable paste.

Divide into 4 portions. Working on a lightly floured board and using floured hands, roll each portion out to a long sausage shape, 1–2 cm ($\frac{1}{2}$–$\frac{3}{4}$ in) in diameter. Cut each sausage into 10 cm (4 in) lengths and twist each into a letter 'S' shape.

Place the jumbles on the prepared trays, spaced well apart. Bake for 15–20 minutes until just turning pale golden. Remove from the oven and leave to cool on the trays for 2–3 minutes before lifting carefully on to a wire rack to cool completely.

INGREDIENTS

100 g (4 oz) butter, softened, plus 10 ml (2 tsp) to grease baking trays

175 g (6 oz) caster sugar

1 medium egg, beaten

$\frac{1}{2}$ tsp almond essence

225 g (8 oz) plain flour, sifted, plus 45–60 ml (3–4 tbsp) to flour hands and board

100 g (4 oz) ground almonds

LEMON CRUMBLE ♦ BISCUITS ♦

The sharp lemony flavour of these biscuits makes them an ideal accompaniment to a cup of tea, particularly Earl Grey or Lapsang Souchong.

♦ **Preparation** 50 minutes ♦ **Cooking** 12–15 minutes ♦ **Makes** 20–22 biscuits ♦

METHOD

Grease 2 large baking trays.

Rub or cut the fat into the flour until the mixture resembles fine breadcrumbs. Add the sugar, egg yolks and lemon rind and mix well with a fork. Using floured hands, knead the mixture to a smooth dough in the bowl. Cover and chill in the refrigerator for 30 minutes.

Heat the oven to 325°F (170°C/Gas 3). Remove the dough from the fridge. Break small pieces off with your hands and roll each into 2$\frac{1}{2}$ cm (1 in) balls. Place these on the prepared trays and flatten them with fork prongs, making a pattern.

Bake the biscuits for 12–15 minutes until very pale golden. Remove from the oven and leave to cool on the trays for 2–3 minutes before carefully lifting on to a wire rack to cool completely.

INGREDIENTS

100 g (4 oz) butter or margarine, softened, plus 10 ml (2 tsp) to grease baking trays

225 g (8 oz) plain flour, sifted, plus 45–60 ml (3–4 tbsp) to flour hands

175 g (6 oz) caster sugar

2 medium egg yolks

Grated rind of 2 lemons

◆ MACAROONS ◆

Easy to make, these have a lovely crisp outside and a chewy middle.

◆ **Preparation** 5 minutes ◆ **Cooking** 20–25 minutes ◆ **Makes** 12–14 biscuits ◆

INGREDIENTS

1 medium egg white
75 g (3 oz) ground almonds
90 g (3½ oz) caster sugar, plus
    45–60 ml (3–4 tbsp) to
    sugar hands
½ tsp almond essence
12–13 split blanched almonds

Pictured opposite page 129

METHOD

Heat the oven to 350°F (180°C/Gas 4) and line a baking tray with
rice paper.

Beat the egg white until stiff and then fold in the ground almonds,
sugar and almond essence. With sugared hands, take teaspoonfuls of the
mixture and roll them between your palms to form small balls.

Place the balls on the rice paper, spaced well apart, and press a
blanched almond into the top of each.

Bake for 20–25 minutes until lightly coloured. Remove from the
oven and leave to cool completely on the baking tray.

◆ OATMEAL COOKIES ◆

*The oatmeal gives these biscuits a distinctive nutty taste and texture.
They are delicious at any time of the day.*

◆ **Preparation** 15 minutes ◆ **Cooking** 8–10 minutes ◆ **Makes** 24–26 biscuits ◆

INGREDIENTS

75 g (3 oz) butter or
    margarine, softened, plus
    15 ml (1 tbsp) to grease
    baking trays
225 g (8 oz) soft brown sugar
2 medium eggs, beaten
5 ml (1 tsp) vanilla essence
175 g (6 oz) plain flour, sifted
¼ tsp salt
½ tsp baking powder
225 g (8 oz) medium oatmeal
45 ml (3 tbsp) demerara sugar

METHOD

Heat the oven to 375°F (190°C/Gas 5) and grease well 2 or 3 large
baking trays.

Cream the fat and sugar together until light and fluffy. Beat the eggs
and vanilla gradually into the mixture, beating hard between each
addition. Using a metal spoon, gradually fold in the flour, salt, baking
powder and oatmeal. Mix thoroughly.

Drop dessertspoonfuls of the mixture on to the prepared trays, spaced
well apart as they spread during cooking. Sprinkle them with the
demerara sugar.

Bake the cookies for 8–10 minutes until golden. Remove from the
oven and leave to cool on the trays for 1 minute before carefully
transferring to a wire rack to cool completely.

◆ SHORTBREAD ◆

Although shortbread is traditionally a Christmas food, it is popular throughout the year. This recipe is for a particularly soft, buttery shortbread.

◆ **Preparation** 10 minutes ◆ **Cooking** 20–25 minutes ◆ **Makes** 16 biscuits ◆

METHOD

Heat the oven to 325°F (170°C/Gas 3) and grease and line 2 × 18 cm (7 in) round sandwich tins, preferably loose-bottomed or with a sliding metal rod to loosen the cakes.

Mix the flour and cornflour together in a bowl. In a separate bowl, cream the butter and sugar together until very light and fluffy. Add the almond essence and beat again. Gradually mix in the flour and cornflour, to make a very light, crumbly mixture.

Divide the mixture between the prepared tins and press down firmly. Smooth the tops very carefully. Mark, do not cut, each into 8 portions and prick a pattern over the top with fork prongs.

Bake for 20–25 minutes until light golden. Remove from the oven and leave to cool in the tins for 5–10 minutes before turning out. To serve, cut or break along the lines marked.

INGREDIENTS

350 g (12 oz) self-raising flour, sifted
100 g (4 oz) cornflour
225 g (8 oz) slightly salted or unsalted butter, plus 10 ml (2 tsp) to grease tins
175 g (6 oz) caster sugar
Few drops of almond essence

◆ SHREWSBURY BISCUITS ◆

These curranty biscuits have a subtle lemony flavour. More lemon peel can be added if you like a sharper taste.

◆ **Preparation** 15 minutes ◆ **Cooking** 15–20 minutes ◆ **Makes** 12–14 biscuits ◆

METHOD

Heat the oven to 350°F (180°C/Gas 4) and grease well a large baking tray.

Cream the fat and sugar together until light and fluffy. Mix in the lemon rind, currants and flour and, using floured hands, knead to a stiff paste in the bowl.

Roll the paste out on a floured board to a thickness of about 5 mm ($\frac{1}{4}$ in). Cut out circles using a 7.5 cm (3 in) cutter dipped in flour. Place the circles carefully on the prepared tray.

Bake for 15–20 minutes until the biscuits are just turning very pale golden. Do not overcook. Remove from the oven and sprinkle immediately with caster sugar. Allow to cool on the tray for 2–3 minutes before lifting the biscuits carefully on to a wire rack to cool completely.

INGREDIENTS

100 g (4 oz) butter or margarine, softened, plus 5 ml (1 tsp) to grease baking tray
100 g (4 oz) caster sugar, plus 30 ml (2 tbsp) to sprinkle biscuits
10 ml (2 tsp) grated lemon rind
50 g (2 oz) currants
175 g (6 oz) plain flour, sifted, plus 45–60 ml (3–4 tbsp) to flour hands and board

Pictured opposite page 49

SMALL CAKES

The recipes in this chapter cover both traditional 'everyday' cakes for family afternoon tea, such as fairy cakes, lemon tarts and Eccles cakes, and more fancy cakes for special teas, such as brandy snaps, cream choux buns and meringues. It may take rather longer to make these more special cakes, but it is well worth the effort as home-made cakes are so much nicer than the shop varieties. The joy is that they can be made as small or as large as required: for instance, meringues can be made bite-sized for elegant afternoon tea or huge, fluffy and full of cream for desserts. Most of the cakes can be cut much smaller to make dainty petits fours.

It is also worth experimenting with fillings. The whipped cream that is piped into the cream slices or brandy snaps can be flavoured with liqueurs; cream choux buns can be filled with almost any fruit and cream or confectioners' custard (see page 69); éclairs can be topped with coffee glacé icing instead of chocolate.

INGREDIENTS

For the pastry
75 g (3 oz) plain flour, sifted
Pinch of salt
25 g (1 oz) caster sugar
50 g (2 oz) margarine or
    butter, softened, plus 5 ml
    (1 tsp) to grease tin

ALMOND & CHERRY
♦ SQUARES ♦

These squares have a pastry base, a middle layer of cherries and a light almond sponge topping.

♦ **Preparation** 15 minutes ♦ **Cooking** 35–40 minutes ♦ **Makes** 16 squares ♦

METHOD

Heat the oven to 375°F (190°C/Gas 5) and grease and line a 20 cm (8 in) square tin.

Mix the flour, salt and sugar together and rub or cut in the fat until the mixture begins to stick together. Press this into the prepared tin and smooth with a palette knife.

Place the cherry halves, flat side down, in neat rows over the top of the pastry, fairly close together.

Cream the margarine and sugar together until light and fluffy. Add the egg and beat well. Beat in the almonds and almond essence. If the mixture is too stiff, add a little milk. Spoon the mixture over the cherries and pastry.

Bake for 35–40 minutes until lightly browned. Remove from the oven and leave to cool in the tin before cutting into 16 squares. Lift the squares carefully on to a wire rack to cool completely.

For the topping
225 g (8 oz) glacé cherries, rinsed, dried and halved
50 g (2 oz) margarine, softened
50 g (2 oz) caster sugar
1 large egg, beaten
50 g (2 oz) ground almonds
½ tsp almond essence
5–10 ml (1–2 tsp) milk, if necessary

◆ BAKEWELL TARTS ◆

These tarts were originally from Bakewell, in Derbyshire. The recipe has gradually changed over the years, and this is the version most people know today.

◆ **Preparation** 30 minutes, plus 20 minutes for pastry ◆ **Cooking** 15–20 minutes ◆
◆ **Makes** 14–16 small or 12 large tarts ◆

METHOD

Make the pastry as on page 139 and chill for 15 minutes.

Heat the oven to 350°F (180°C/Gas 4) and grease 14–16 small or 12 deep patty tins.

For the filling, cream the fat and sugar together until light and fluffy. Beat in the egg and almond essence. Fold in the flour and ground almonds with a metal spoon and mix thoroughly.

Roll out the pastry on a floured board to a thickness of 5 mm (¼ in). Cut out 14–16 circles using a 7.5 cm (3 in) cutter dipped in flour, or 12 circles using a 10 cm (4 in) cutter dipped in flour.

Line the prepared tins with the circles of pastry. Put a heaped teaspoonful of jam into the base of each tart and drop spoonfuls of the filling on top.

Bake the tarts for 15–20 minutes until well risen and golden. Remove from the oven and decorate each with a half glacé cherry. Cool the tarts in the tins for 5–10 minutes before transferring them to a wire rack to cool completely.

INGREDIENTS
1 quantity shortcrust pastry, using 225 g (8 oz) flour (see page 139)
50 g (2 oz) margarine or butter, softened, plus 15 ml (1 tbsp) to grease tins
50 g (2 oz) caster sugar
1 large egg, beaten
½ tsp almond essence
30 g (1½ oz) self-raising flour, sifted, plus 50–75 g (2–3 oz) to flour board
15 g (½ oz) ground almonds
About 150 g (5 oz) raspberry or strawberry jam
6–8 glacé cherries, halved

INGREDIENTS

For the brandy snaps
25 g (1 oz) butter or
   margarine, softened, plus
   10 ml (2 tsp) to grease
   baking trays
65 g (2½ oz) caster sugar
22 ml (1½ tbsp) syrup
25 g (1 oz) plain flour, sifted,
   plus 45–60 ml (3–4 tbsp) to
   flour hands
5 ml (1 tsp) ground ginger

For the filling
275 ml (½ pt) double cream
14 pieces of crystallized
   ginger

Pictured opposite page 81

◆ BRANDY SNAPS ◆

*There is quite a knack in catching these at just the right temperature to
wind them around the wooden spoons. The winding has to be done
while the mixture is still pliable but firm enough to hold the shape. You
will need about 4 wooden spoons ready.*

◆ **Preparation** 10 minutes ◆ **Cooking** 10–12 minutes ◆ **Makes** 14 snaps ◆

METHOD

Heat the oven to 300°F (150°C/Gas 2) and grease 2 large baking trays.

Cream the fat, sugar and syrup together until light and fluffy. Stir in
the flour and ginger. Using floured hands, roll the mixture into 14 small
balls and place well apart on the prepared trays. They spread while
cooking so leave plenty of room.

Bake for 10–12 minutes until rich brown. Remove from the oven
and leave to cool slightly. Remove from the baking trays with a palette
knife, and while still hot, wind them around the handles of wooden
spoons, about 3–4 on each handle. Leave to set on a work surface or
board. This will take 5–10 minutes. When the snaps are set, slide them
off the wooden spoons and place on a wire rack to cool completely.

Whip the cream until stiff and place in a piping bag. Fill each brandy
snap with cream and place a piece of crystallized ginger on one end of
each snap to decorate.

INGREDIENTS

100 g (4 oz) self-raising flour,
   sifted
50 g (2 oz) cocoa powder
100 g (4 oz) margarine,
   softened, plus 5 ml (1 tsp)
   to grease tin
225 g (8 oz) soft brown sugar
2 medium eggs, beaten
150 ml (¼ pt) milk
5 ml (1 tsp) vanilla essence
100 g (4 oz) chopped walnuts
100 g (4 oz) raisins

Pictured opposite page 96

◆ CHOCOLATE SQUARES ◆

These delicious gooey squares contain raisins and walnuts.

◆ **Preparation** 10 minutes ◆ **Cooking** 30 minutes ◆ **Makes** 16 squares ◆

METHOD

Heat the oven to 325°F (180°C/Gas 3) and grease and line a 20 cm
(8 in) square tin.

Mix the flour and cocoa together in a bowl. In a separate bowl, cream
the margarine and sugar together until light and fluffy. Gradually add
the eggs, a little at a time, beating hard between each addition.
Gradually mix in the flour and cocoa, beating in a little of the milk
between each addition. Stir in the vanilla, nuts and raisins.

Pour into the prepared tin and bake for 30 minutes until risen and
firm on top. Remove from the oven and leave to cool in the tin. Do not
attempt to cut it until quite cold, or the meringue-like topping will
crumble badly. When cold, cut into 16 squares and remove carefully
from the tin.

♦ CREAM CHOUX BUNS ♦

Other fruit can be used instead of strawberries or raspberries. Pineapple or peaches are excellent alternatives, or a good fruit preserve can be used. The choux pastry needs to be freshly made for this recipe.

♦ **Preparation** 15–20 minutes, including pastry ♦ **Cooking** 40 minutes ♦
♦ **Makes** 24 small or 12 large buns ♦

METHOD

Heat the oven to 400°F (200°C/Gas 6) and grease a large baking tray.

Make the pastry as on page 136. While the dough is still tepid, put it in a piping bag with a 2.5 cm (1 in) star nozzle, and pipe 24 small or 12 large balls on to the prepared tray.

Bake for 30 minutes, making sure that you do not open the oven door during that time. Reduce the heat to 325°F (170°C/Gas 3) and bake for a further 10 minutes. Cover with greaseproof paper if the pastry is becoming too brown.

Remove from the oven, split the buns horizontally, open and remove any damp dough. Switch off the oven. If the buns are still very damp inside, put them back in the switched-off oven to dry out.

Whip the cream until very stiff. Gradually whip in the kirsch and the sugar. When the buns are cold, spoon in the whipped cream and lay the fruit on top. Dredge the top of each bun with icing sugar.

INGREDIENTS

5 ml (1 tsp) margarine, to grease baking tray
1 quantity choux pastry, using 100 g (4 oz) flour (see page 136)
275 ml ($\frac{1}{2}$ pt) double cream
15 ml (1 tbsp) kirsch
15 ml (1 tbsp) caster sugar
450 g (1 lb) fresh strawberries or raspberries, hulled and halved
45–60 ml (3–4 tbsp) icing sugar

Pictured opposite page 65

♦ CREAM SLICES ♦

Jam or fresh fruit can be used in these slices, and the tops can be dusted with icing sugar instead of glacé icing, if preferred.

♦ **Preparation** 30 minutes, plus 4 hours for pastry ♦ **Cooking** 8–10 minutes ♦
♦ **Makes** 10 slices ♦

METHOD

Make the pastry as on page 137 and chill for 30 minutes.

Heat the oven to 425°F (220°C/Gas 7) and grease 2 baking trays. Sprinkle the trays with a little water.

Roll out the pastry on a floured board to a thin sheet. Prick all over with a fork and cut into 15 slices, each 10 × 6 cm (4 × 2$\frac{1}{2}$ in).

Place the pastry slices on the prepared trays and bake for 8–10 minutes until light golden. Remove from the oven and transfer to a wire rack to cool. When cold, split each pastry slice horizontally across the middle.

Mix the icing sugar with the water. Put a little of the icing, about 45–60 ml (3–4 tbsp), to one side and, with a palette knife, spread the rest

INGREDIENTS

$\frac{1}{4}$ quantity puff pastry, using 100 g (4 oz) flour (see page 137)
10 ml (2 tsp) margarine, to grease baking trays
50–75 g (2–3 oz) flour, to flour board
225 g (8 oz) icing sugar
15 ml (1 tbsp) water
Few drops of pink food colouring
275 ml ($\frac{1}{2}$ pt) double cream
About 50 g (2 oz) strawberry or raspberry jam, or 100 g (4 oz) fresh fruit, prepared and sliced

Pictured opposite page 65

Continued overleaf

over the undersides of 10 of the pastry pieces. Leave on a wire rack to set, with the icing sides uppermost.

Add 3–4 drops of pink food colouring to the remaining icing and put into a piping bag with a very small, plain nozzle. Pipe 3 thin pink lines lengthways over the white icing of each slice, and then draw a skewer gently from side to side through the lines to create a decorative marbled effect.

Whip the cream until stiff. Spread 10 of the pastry slices with jam or with pieces of fresh fruit. Spread the whipped cream on top. Lay the remaining 10 pastry slices on top and add another layer of jam or fruit and cream. Lay the iced pieces of pastry on top of the jam and cream and serve immediately.

◆ ECCLES CAKES ◆

Eccles cakes are traditional cakes very similar to Banbury cakes, Coventry God cakes, Hawkshead cakes and Chorley cakes. All are of the same family, but vary in shape. Chorley cakes are round, Hawkshead cakes are as large as a plate, Coventry God cakes are in the shape of an isosceles triangle and Banbury cakes are oval. These Eccles cakes are small and round.

◆ **Preparation** 20–25 minutes, plus 2 hours for pastry ◆ **Cooking** 10–15 minutes ◆
◆ **Makes** 12 cakes ◆

INGREDIENTS

$\frac{1}{4}$ quantity flaky pastry, using 100 g (4 oz) flour (see page 137)
50–75 g (2–3 oz) flour, to flour board
25 g (1 oz) butter, softened, plus 10 ml (2 tsp) to grease baking trays
25 g (1 oz) soft brown sugar
25 g (1 oz) mixed candied peel
75 g (3 oz) currants
1 medium egg white, beaten
30 ml (2 tbsp) caster sugar

Pictured opposite page 96

METHOD

Make the pastry as on page 137 and chill for 1 hour.

Roll out the pastry on a floured board. Cut out 12 circles using a 10 cm (4 in) cutter dipped in flour. If you cannot buy a cutter this size, use the rim of a thin-edged bowl or cup.

Cream the butter and sugar together in a bowl until light and fluffy, and mix in the candied peel and currants. Place teaspoonfuls of the currant mixture in the middle of each circle of pastry. Dampen the edges of the pastry with water and close them up over the middle. Press well together. Turn over so that the join is underneath. Grease 2 large baking trays.

On a floured board, roll out each filled ball of pastry to a thickness of 10 mm ($\frac{1}{3}$ in) so that the currants just show. Place on the prepared trays and chill for 10–15 minutes. Meanwhile, heat the oven to 450°F (230°C/Gas 8).

Make 3 slits across the top of each Eccles cake, brush them all over with the beaten egg white and dredge with the sugar. Bake for 10–15 minutes until pale golden and crisp. Remove from the oven and transfer to a wire rack to cool.

♦ ÉCLAIRS ♦

The trick of cooking éclairs is to dampen one side of the greaseproof paper on which they are cooked, as the steam helps the pastry to rise and puff up. The choux pastry needs to be freshly made for this recipe.

♦ **Preparation** 30 minutes, including pastry ♦ **Cooking** 25–30 minutes ♦
♦ **Makes** 14 éclairs ♦

INGREDIENTS

1 quantity choux pastry, using 100 g (4 oz) flour (see page 136)
275 ml (½ pt) double cream
175 g (6 oz) plain chocolate
25 g (1 oz) butter

Pictured opposite page 97

METHOD

Heat the oven to 400°F (200°C/Gas 6). Cut out 2 pieces of greaseproof paper to fit 2 large baking trays. Dampen one side of each piece of paper and lay, wet side down, on the trays.

Make the choux pastry as on page 136. While the dough is still tepid, put it in a piping bag with a 1 cm (½ in) plain nozzle, and pipe into 14 × 10 cm (4 in) lengths on the prepared trays.

Bake for 25–30 minutes until crisp and brown, making sure that you do not open the oven door during that time. Remove from the oven and immediately make a slit along one side of each éclair to let the steam escape. Transfer to a wire rack to cool completely.

Whip the cream until very stiff and put into a piping bag. Pipe the cream into the éclairs.

Melt the chocolate and butter together in a shallow bowl set over a saucepan of simmering water. Stir continuously. Dip the top of each éclair into the chocolate, turn back upright and leave on a wire rack for the chocolate topping to set.

♦ FAIRY CAKES ♦

These cakes can be decorated in a variety of ways. Try the suggestions here or use your own favourite icing ideas.

♦ **Preparation** 30 minutes ♦ **Cooking** 10 minutes ♦ **Makes** 12 cakes ♦

INGREDIENTS

For the cakes
50 g (2 oz) margarine, softened
50 g (2 oz) caster sugar
1 large egg, beaten
100 g (4 oz) self-raising flour, sifted
15 ml (1 tbsp) boiling water

METHOD

Heat the oven to 400°F (200°C/Gas 2) and place 12 paper cake cases in bun tins.

Cream the margarine and sugar together until light and fluffy. Add the egg and beat very well. Fold in the flour and beat again, then beat the boiling water well into the mixture. Spoon the cake mixture into the paper cases.

Bake for 10 minutes until golden. Remove from the oven and leave to cool. When cool, remove the cakes from the tins, still in their cases, and place on a plate to decorate.

Continued overleaf

For the decoration
50 g (2 oz) butter, softened
100 g (4 oz) icing sugar
15–30 ml (1–2 tbsp) milk or
    top of the milk
10 ml (2 tsp) raspberry or
    strawberry jam
5 ml (1 tsp) freshly squeezed
    lemon juice
5 ml (1 tsp) grated lemon rind
8 lemon or orange candy
    slices, or strips of lemon or
    orange zest
5 ml (1 tsp) cocoa powder
8 chocolate buttons

TO DECORATE

First cream the butter with the icing sugar until light and fluffy. Add the milk and continue beating until the icing is smooth and well blended. Divide into 3 equal portions. Mix 1 portion with the raspberry or strawberry preserve, mix another portion with the lemon juice and a little finely grated lemon rind, and mix the remaining portion with the cocoa.

To make 4 butterfly fairy cakes, first cut out a small circle from the top of 4 cakes. Slice each circle in half to make semi-circles. Fill the hollow in the top of the cakes with the raspberry or strawberry butter icing, and place the semi-circles, cut side down, at an angle in the top of the icing to form butterfly wings.

To make 4 lemon fairy cakes, first ice the tops of 4 cakes with the lemon butter icing. Decorate the top of each with lemon and orange slices, or with strips of fresh lemon or orange zest.

To make 4 chocolate fairy cakes, first ice the tops of the cakes with the cocoa butter icing. Decorate the top of each with 2 chocolate buttons, placed at an angle in the icing.

INGREDIENTS

½ quantity shortcrust pastry,
    using 100 g (4 oz) flour (see
    page 139)
50–75 g (2–3 oz) flour, to
    flour board
50 g (2 oz) butter, softened,
    plus 10 ml (2 tsp) to grease
    tins
50 g (2 oz) caster sugar
1 medium egg, beaten
15 ml (1 tbsp) plain flour,
    sifted
50 g (2 oz) ground almonds
2–3 drops of almond essence
About 40 split almonds
30 ml (2 tbsp) apricot jam
10 ml (2 tsp) water

Pictured opposite page 17

♦ FRANGIPANI TARTS ♦

These little almond tarts are a pretty addition to a tea table. If you have them, use wavy-edged cutters.

♦ **Preparation** 20–25 minutes, plus 20 minutes for pastry ♦ **Cooking** 20 minutes ♦
♦ **Makes** 10 tarts ♦

METHOD

Make the pastry as on page 139 and chill for 15 minutes.

Heat the oven to 400°F (200°C/Gas 6) and grease 10 patty tins.

Roll out the pastry thinly on a floured board. Cut out 10 circles using a 7.5 cm (3 in) cutter dipped in flour, and use these to line the prepared tins. Chill for 15 minutes.

Meanwhile, cream the butter and sugar together until light and fluffy. Beat in the egg thoroughly and then beat in the flour, almonds and almond essence. Spoon the mixture into the prepared pastry cases, each about two-thirds full. Arrange about 4 split almonds on top of each.

Bake for 20 minutes until golden. Meanwhile, heat the jam with the water in a saucepan to make the glaze. Bring to the boil and then sieve and reheat. Remove the tarts from the oven and immediately brush them all over with the glaze. Transfer the tarts carefully to a wire rack to cool.

Small cakes Top left: Maids of honour (see page 67); Top right: Nut cherry shortcake (see page 68); Centre: Strawberry tarts (see page 69); Bottom: Lemon grape slices (see page 65).

◆ LEMON GRAPE SLICES ◆

These are impressive enough to serve as a dessert at a dinner party. The creamy lemon custard is an excellent contrast to the light puff pastry.

◆ **Preparation** 30 minutes, plus 4 hours for pastry ◆ **Cooking** 10–15 minutes ◆
◆ **Makes** 7 slices ◆

METHOD

Make the pastry as on page 137 and chill for 30 minutes.

Heat the oven to 450°F (230°C/Gas 8) and grease a large baking tray. Roll out the pastry on a floured board to a rectangle, 35 × 20 cm (14 × 8 in). Cut into 14 slices by cutting down the middle of the rectangle lengthways and then crossways into 7 strips, 5 cm (2 in) wide.

Place the slices on the prepared tray and bake for 10–15 minutes until well risen and golden. Remove from the oven and transfer to a wire rack to cool.

Meanwhile, in a small saucepan, mix together the cornflour, sugar and milk and bring slowly to the boil, stirring all the time, until it thickens. Stir in the lemon juice and rind. Add the egg yolk and beat thoroughly. Take off the heat and leave until cold. Beat in the cream.

Keep back 14 grapes for decoration. Halve and pip the rest, and mix into the lemon sauce.

Take 7 of the pastry slices and turn them upside-down. Spread a layer of the grape and lemon sauce on top of each, and then place the other 7 pastry slices on top. Mix together the icing sugar and water and spread over the top of each slice with a palette knife.

Beat the egg white until stiff. Dip the reserved 14 grapes into the egg white and then into the extra caster sugar. Leave to dry and then arrange 2 grapes on top of each slice.

INGREDIENTS

½ quantity puff pastry, using 225 g (8 oz) flour (see page 137)
5 ml (1 tsp) margarine, to grease baking tray
50–75 g (2–3 oz) flour, to flour board
25 g (1 oz) cornflour
40 g (1½ oz) caster sugar, plus 30 ml (2 tbsp) to coat grapes
150 ml (¼ pt) milk
Juice of 1 lemon
Grated rind of ½ lemon
1 medium egg, separated
60 ml (4 tbsp) double cream
150 g (5 oz) green or white grapes
100 g (4 oz) icing sugar
15–30 ml (1–2 tbsp) water

Pictured opposite page 64

◆ LEMON MERINGUE FINGERS ◆

These combine a rich lemony sponge with a frothy meringue topping.

◆ **Preparation** 15 minutes ◆ **Cooking** 40–45 minutes ◆
◆ **Makes** 12 small or 8 large fingers ◆

METHOD

Heat the oven to 325°F (170°C/Gas 3) and grease and line a 20 cm (8 in) square tin.

Cream the fat and sugar together until light and fluffy. Beat in the egg yolks, lemon rind and juice. Add the flour and mix to a stiff dough

INGREDIENTS

100 g (4 oz) butter or margarine, softened, plus 5 ml (1 tsp) to grease tin
100 g (4 oz) caster sugar
3 medium eggs, separated
Grated rind of 1 lemon
10 ml (2 tsp) freshly squeezed lemon juice

Continued overleaf

Afternoon tea Clockwise from top: Special chocolate cake (see page 81); Cream choux buns (see page 61); Cream slices (see page 61); Meringues Marguerite (see page 115).

225 g (8 oz) self-raising flour,
  sifted
75 g (3 oz) chopped walnuts
175 g (6 oz) icing sugar

Pictured opposite page 17

with a fork. Press the mixture into the prepared tin and level with a palette knife. Sprinkle over the nuts.

Beat the egg whites until stiff. Beat in half the icing sugar, a little at a time. Then fold in all except 1 tablespoonful of the remaining icing sugar. Spread over the nuts and dough, pulling at the meringue with a knife blade to peak it. Sprinkle over the rest of the icing sugar.

Bake for 40–45 minutes until pale golden. Remove from the oven and leave to cool in the tin. When cold, cut carefully into 12 small or 8 large fingers.

◆ LEMON TARTS ◆

The filling for these tarts can also be used as lemon curd for spreading on breads and scones.

◆ **Preparation** 30 minutes, plus 10 minutes for pastry ◆ **Cooking** 10–15 minutes ◆
◆ **Makes** 20 tarts ◆

INGREDIENTS

½ quantity rich shortcrust
  pastry, using 100 g (4 oz)
  flour (see page 138)
Grated rind and juice of 2
  lemons
50 g (2 oz) butter
2 medium eggs, lightly
  beaten
225 g (8 oz) caster sugar
15 ml (1 tbsp) margarine, to
  grease tins
50–75 g (2–3 oz) flour, to
  flour board
20 lemon or orange candy
  slices, or strips of lemon
  and orange rind, to
  decorate tarts

METHOD

Make the pastry as on page 138 and chill for 15 minutes while you make the filling.

Place the lemon rind, juice, butter, eggs and sugar into a double boiler or in a bowl set over a saucepan of simmering water. Cook, stirring frequently, until the mixture thickens. Leave to cool.

Heat the oven to 400°F (200°C/Gas 6) and grease 20 bun tins.

Roll out the pastry on a floured board and cut out 20 circles using a 7.5 cm (3 in) cutter dipped in flour. Use these to line the prepared tins. Place a small circle of greaseproof paper in the middle of each, and place a few dried baking beans on top of each piece of paper to stop the pastry base from rising.

Bake blind for 10–15 minutes. Remove from the oven, take out the beans and paper, and leave the tarts to cool in the tins. When cool, transfer to a serving dish.

Put the lemon filling into a piping bag with a 5 mm (¼ in) star nozzle, and pipe the filling into the tart cases. (This can be done with a spoon but you do not get the same decorative effect.) Decorate each tart with the lemon or orange candy slices, or with curled strips of lemon and orange rind.

♦ MAIDS OF HONOUR ♦

These little tartlets, for which there are several different recipes, are said to have been favourites of Anne Boleyn and her Maids of Honour. If you have tiny cutters, use these for a very pretty effect.

♦ **Preparation** 25 minutes, plus 10 minutes for pastry ♦ **Cooking** 35–40 minutes ♦
♦ **Makes** 24–36 tarts, depending on the size of cutter ♦

METHOD

Make the pastry as on page 138 and chill for at least 15 minutes.

Heat the oven to 350°F (180°C/Gas 4) and grease 24 bun tins.

Roll out the pastry on a floured board and cut out 24 circles using a 7.5 cm (3 in) cutter dipped in flour. Use these to line the prepared tins.

Beat together the curd cheese and butter in a bowl. Add the eggs, brandy and sugar and beat again. In a separate bowl, beat the mashed potato, almonds, nutmeg, lemon rind and lemon juice together and then gradually mix in the curd cheese mixture. Beat thoroughly. Spoon the mixture into the pastry cases.

Bake the tarts for 35–40 minutes until firm. Remove from the oven and leave to cool in the tins for 2–3 minutes before transferring carefully to a wire rack to cool completely.

INGREDIENTS

Double quantity rich
   shortcrust pastry, using
   450 g (1 lb) flour (see page
   138)
50–75 g (2–3 oz) flour, to
   flour board
100 g (4 oz) curd cheese,
   softened
75 g (3 oz) butter, softened,
   plus 15 ml (1 tbsp) to grease
   tins
2 medium eggs, beaten
65 ml (2½ fl oz) brandy
75 g (3 oz) caster sugar
75 g (3 oz) cold mashed
   potato
25 g (1 oz) ground almonds
½ tsp ground nutmeg
Grated rind of 2 lemons
Juice of 1 lemon

Pictured opposite page 64

♦ MERINGUES ♦

When beating egg whites it is vital that the bowl you use is free from grease. Serve meringues as soon as possible after making.

♦ **Preparation** 10 minutes ♦ **Cooking** 4–5 hours ♦ **Makes** 10–12 meringues ♦

METHOD

Heat the oven to the lowest possible setting, about 225°F (110°C/Gas ¼). Line 2 large baking trays with greaseproof paper and oil lightly.

Beat the egg whites with the salt until they are stiff and dry, and peak when the beater is lifted. Mix in half the sugar, beating thoroughly. Fold in the rest of the sugar with a metal spoon.

Place heaped teaspoonfuls of the mixture on the oiled paper, about 10–12. Place in the oven and bake for 4–5 hours. Transfer carefully to and airtight container until needed.

Just before serving, whip the cream until stiff. Put in a piping bag with a 1 cm (½ in) star nozzle and pipe on to a meringue. Sandwich together with another meringue and place in a paper case. Repeat for the other meringues. Sprinkle chocolate strands or chopped nuts over the cream to decorate.

INGREDIENTS

For the meringues
15 ml (1 tbsp) vegetable oil, to
   grease paper
2 medium egg whites
Pinch of salt
100 g (4 oz) caster sugar

For the filling
150 ml (¼ pt) double cream
Chocolate strands or chopped
   nuts

INGREDIENTS

For the shortcake
175 g (6 oz) plain flour, sifted
50 g (2 oz) caster sugar
5 ml (1 tsp) ground nutmeg
100 g (4 oz) margarine,
  softened, plus 5 ml (1 tsp)
  to grease tin

For the topping
50 g (2 oz) hazelnuts, chopped
  roughly
75 g (3 oz) glacé cherries, cut
  into quarters
45 ml (3 tbsp) thick honey

Pictured opposite page 64

◆ NUT CHERRY SHORTCAKE ◆

*A brightly coloured nut and cherry topping on a plain shortcake base
makes this a very appetizing and attractive cake at tea time.*

◆ **Preparation** 10 minutes ◆ **Cooking** 30–35 minutes ◆ **Makes** 8 pieces ◆

METHOD

Heat the oven to 325°F (170°C/Gas 3) and grease an 18 cm (7 in)
round sandwich tin.

Mix together the flour, sugar and nutmeg and rub or cut in the
margarine until the mixture begins to stick together. Press into the
prepared tin and smooth the top with a palette knife.

Bake for 30–35 minutes until lightly browned, then remove from the
oven and leave to cool.

Put the nuts, cherries and honey in a small saucepan. Bring to the
boil, stir thoroughly and allow to simmer for 2 minutes until sticky and
beginning to thicken. Spread the mixture evenly over the top of the
shortbread and leave to cool. When the topping has set, cut the
shortcake into 8 pieces.

INGREDIENTS

For the filling
225 g (8 oz) pitted dried dates,
  chopped
150 ml ($\frac{1}{4}$ pt) water
30 ml (2 tbsp) soft brown
  sugar
Juice of 1 lemon
Grated rind of 2 lemons

For the oat pastry
150 g (5 oz) plain flour, sifted
5 ml (1 tsp) bicarbonate of
  soda
125 g (4$\frac{1}{2}$ oz) jumbo rolled
  oats
200 g (7 oz) soft brown sugar
175 g (6 oz) butter, melted,
  plus 30 ml (2 tbsp) to grease
  tins
Juice of 1 lemon

◆ PARK PIES ◆

*Do use plenty of lemon juice in the filling of these pies, as the dates and
oaty case would be too sweet without a strong lemony tang.*

◆ **Preparation** 15–20 minutes ◆ **Cooking** 30 minutes ◆ **Makes** 16 pies ◆

METHOD

Heat the oven to 375°F (190°C/Gas 5) and grease 16 deep patty tins,
each 7.5 cm (3 in) across.

First make the filling. Place the dates, water, sugar, lemon juice and
rind in a small saucepan. Bring to the boil and simmer gently,
uncovered, stirring occasionally until thick and smooth but not dry. If
necessary, add a little more water. Remove from the heat and cool.

Mix together the flour, soda, oats and sugar. Add the melted butter
and lemon juice, and mix with a fork or with floured hands until the
mixture binds together.

Reserve a third of the oat mixture and line the base and sides of the
prepared tins with the rest, pressing well into the tins. Put a generous
teaspoonful of the filling into each tin. Use the remaining third of the
oat mixture to cover the fillings.

Bake the pies for 30 minutes until lightly browned. Remove from the
oven and leave to cool in the tins for 10–15 minutes before lifting
carefully on to a wire rack to cool completely.

♦ QUEEN CAKES ♦

This is an old, traditional English recipe, with the unusual addition of cream to the sponge.

♦ **Preparation** 5 minutes ♦ **Cooking** 20–25 minutes ♦ **Makes** 18 cakes ♦

METHOD

Heat the oven to 375°F (190°C/Gas 5). Place 18 paper cases in bun tins.

Cream the fat and sugar together until light and fluffy. Add the cream and lemon juice and beat thoroughly. Beat in the eggs, one at a time. Add the flour, baking powder, currants and a little milk and beat well.

Spoon the mixture into the paper cases and bake for 20–25 minutes until golden. Remove from the oven and leave in the tins to cool.

INGREDIENTS

100 g (4 oz) butter or
  margarine, softened
100 g (4 oz) caster sugar
22 ml (1½ tbsp) double cream
5 ml (1 tsp) freshly squeezed
  lemon juice
2 medium eggs, beaten
225 g (8 oz) plain flour, sifted
½ tsp baking powder
100 g (4 oz) currants
8–15 ml (½–1 tbsp) milk

♦ STRAWBERRY TARTS ♦

These tarts can be filled with any fresh soft fruit, for example loganberries or raspberries. Fresh whipped cream can also be used instead of the confectioners' custard, if desired.

♦ **Preparation** 30 minutes, plus 25 minutes for pastry ♦ **Cooking** 10 minutes ♦
♦ **Makes** 12 tarts ♦

METHOD

Make the pastry as on page 138 and chill for 15 minutes.

Heat the oven to 375°F (190°C/Gas 5) and grease 12 large patty tins.

Roll out the pastry very thinly on a floured board and cut out 12 circles using a 10 cm (4 in) cutter dipped in flour. Use to line the prepared tins. Place a circle of greaseproof paper in the middle of each and place a few dried baking beans on top.

Bake the tarts blind for 10 minutes until pale golden. Remove from the oven, take out the beans and paper and leave to cool in the tins. When cool, transfer carefully to a serving plate or wire tray.

To make the custard, dissolve the cornflour in a little of the milk in a saucepan. Gradually stir in the rest of the milk, the sugar, and the egg or egg yolks. Bring slowly to the boil, stirring all the time. Allow to thicken, then remove from the heat, add the essence and stir thoroughly. Leave to cool. Sprinkle a little caster sugar all over the surface to stop a skin forming.

When the custard is cold, beat hard and spoon into the tart cases. Arrange the strawberries neatly over the custard.

Heat the redcurrant jelly with the water in a saucepan to make the glaze. Bring to the boil and then sieve and reheat. Brush the glaze all over the strawberries to seal them. Leave to set before serving.

INGREDIENTS

For the pastry
¼ quantity rich shortcrust
  pastry, using 100 g (4 oz)
  flour (see page 138)
10 ml (2 tsp) margarine, to
  grease tins
50–75 g (2–3 oz) flour, to
  flour board

For the confectioners' custard
20 g (¾ oz) cornflour
275 ml (½ pt) milk
50 g (2 oz) caster sugar, plus
  45–60 ml (3–4 tbsp) to
  sprinkle tarts
1 medium egg or 2 egg yolks,
  beaten
6–7 drops of almond essence

For the topping
450 g (1 lb) fresh strawberries,
  hulled and halved
75 ml (5 tbsp) redcurrant jelly
22 ml (1½ tbsp) water

Pictured opposite page 64

FAMILY & SEASONAL CAKES

Most of the recipes in this chapter are for everyday teas and high teas. Some, for example the mincemeat cake and the chocolate cake, are fancier than others and can be made for slightly more special occasions. Others, such as the Christmas cake, Whitby yule cake and simnel cake, are traditional cakes for particular festivals.

For most seasonal occasions it is possible to create a suitable cake by icing and decorating a plain sponge or fruit cake (for instance the victoria sponge or family fruit cake) appropriately. For an Easter cake, ice a cake with yellow and white icing and decorate it with spring flowers, Easter chicks and sugar eggs. For birthdays, the cake can be iced in the person's favourite colour, and lettering and motifs piped on top.

INGREDIENTS

100 g (4 oz) butter, melted, plus 5 ml (1 tsp) to grease tin

275 g (10 oz) self-raising flour, sifted

12.5 ml (2½ tsp) ground cinnamon

5 ml (1 tsp) ground mixed spice

½ tsp salt

225 g (8 oz) demerara sugar

75 g (3 oz) raisins

2 large eggs, beaten

175 ml (6 fl oz) milk

225 g (8 oz) apples, peeled, cored and grated

30 ml (2 tbsp) caster sugar

◆ APPLE & SPICE CAKE ◆

The best apples for this cake would be a crisp, sharply flavoured eating variety. Do not use cooking apples as they are too sour.

◆ **Preparation** 10–15 minutes ◆ **Cooking** 1–1¼ hours ◆ **Makes** 20 cm (8 in) square cake ◆

METHOD

Heat the oven to 350°F (180°C/Gas 4) and grease and line a 20 cm (8 in) square tin.

Put all the ingredients except the caster sugar in a bowl and mix gradually to blend. Beat well for 2–3 minutes and turn into the prepared tin.

Bake for 1–1¼ hours until dark golden and firm to the touch. Test with a skewer. Remove from the oven and leave to cool in the tin for 10–15 minutes before turning out on to a wire rack to cool completely. Put on to a serving plate and dredge the top with the caster sugar.

♦ BANANA & CHERRY CAKE ♦

This is an excellent way of using up over-ripe bananas. The cake is very moist, and the wholewheat flour gives it a nutty texture.

♦ **Preparation** 10 minutes ♦ **Cooking** 1¼–1½ hours ♦
♦ **Makes** 18 cm (7 in) round cake or 900 g (2 lb) loaf ♦

METHOD

Heat the oven to 325°F (170°C/Gas 3) and grease and line an 18 cm (7 in) round tin or a 900 g (2 lb) loaf tin.

Put all the ingredients in a bowl and beat thoroughly to blend well together. Beat for a further 2 minutes to incorporate air into the mixture and turn into the prepared tin. Make a small dip in the middle of the cake, as it tends to rise.

Bake for 1¼–1½ hours until brown and firm. Test with a skewer. Remove from the oven and leave to cool in the tin for 15 minutes before turning out on to a wire rack to cool completely.

INGREDIENTS

100 g (4 oz) margarine or butter, softened, plus 5 ml (1 tsp) to grease tin
100 g (4 oz) glacé cherries, quartered
2 ripe bananas, mashed
225 g (8 oz) plain wholewheat flour, sifted
Pinch of salt
175 g (6 oz) soft brown sugar
2 large eggs, beaten

Pictured opposite page 80

CHOCOLATE CINNAMON ♦ ROLL ♦

This large roll can be served as a sumptuous dessert as well as at tea time.

♦ **Preparation** 25 minutes ♦ **Cooking** 7–9 minutes ♦ **Makes** 23 cm (9 in) roll ♦

METHOD

Heat the oven to 425°F (225°C/Gas 7) and grease and line a 33 × 23 cm (13 × 9 in) Swiss roll tin.

Beat the eggs and sugar together in a bowl set over a saucepan of simmering water until the mixture leaves a trail when the beater is lifted. Using a metal spoon, carefully fold in the flour, cinnamon, cocoa and salt. Add the hot water and stir carefully, making sure that all the ingredients are well blended.

Pour into the prepared tin and bake for 7–9 minutes until firm. Have ready a sheet of greaseproof paper. Place it on top of a damp cloth and sprinkle with the extra 30 ml (2 tbsp) caster sugar.

Remove the cake from the oven and turn immediately on to the sugared paper. Peel off the lining paper. While still hot, trim the edges of the cake and roll up with the sugared paper to cool.

Whip the cream until firm, and gradually beat in the kirsch. Gently unroll the cake and spread with the cream. Roll up again without the paper, and hold in place for a few minutes. Dredge the roll with icing sugar and make a pattern of criss–cross lines with a hot skewer.

INGREDIENTS

For the roll
5 ml (1 tsp) margarine, to grease tin
3 medium eggs, beaten
100 g (4 oz) caster sugar, plus 30 ml (2 tbsp) to sugar paper
75 g (3 oz) plain flour, sifted
5 ml (1 tsp) ground cinnamon
25 g (1 oz) cocoa powder
Good pinch of salt
15 ml (1 tbsp) hot water

For the filling
175 ml (6 fl oz) double cream
22 ml (1½ tbsp) kirsch
30 ml (2 tbsp) icing sugar

Pictured opposite page 80

INGREDIENTS

For the cake

225 g (8 oz) butter, softened,
    plus 30 ml (2 tbsp) to grease
    tin and paper
225 g (8 oz) soft brown sugar,
    rolled out to remove any
    lumps
4 large eggs, beaten
10 ml (2 tsp) black treacle
100 ml (4 fl oz) medium
    sherry
½ tsp vanilla essence
¼ tsp almond essence
100 g (4 oz) plain flour, sifted
175 g (6 oz) self-raising flour,
    sifted
¼ tsp salt
5 ml (1 tsp) ground cinnamon
½ tsp ground nutmeg
5 ml (1 tsp) ground mixed
    spice
350 g (12 oz) raisins
450 g (1 lb) sultanas
450 g (1 lb) currants
75 g (3 oz) glacé cherries,
    quartered
100 g (4 oz) mixed candied
    peel
50 g (2 oz) chopped blanched
    almonds or walnuts
50 g (2 oz) ground almonds

For the marzipan

175 g (6 oz) icing sugar and
    175 g (6 oz) caster sugar,
    OR 350 g (12 oz) icing
    sugar, plus 45–60 ml
    (3–4 tbsp) to sugar board
350 g (12 oz) ground almonds
Juice of ½ lemon
3–4 drops of almond essence
1–2 medium egg yolks,
    beaten

Pictured opposite page 81

◆ CHRISTMAS CAKE ◆

*This is my personal favourite. It is an old recipe of my mother's, and
gives a rich, moist but not bitter cake. Like most fruit cakes it is best
made 5–6 weeks before eating.*

◆ **Cooking times for different shapes and sizes** ◆
18 cm (7 in) square tin: same quantity for 3¼–3½ hours
20 cm (8 in) square tin: same quantity for 3 hours
15 cm (6 in) round tin: ½ quantity for 2½–2¾ hours
18 cm (7 in) round tin: ½ quantity for 3½ hours

◆ **Preparation** 50–60 minutes, plus 4–6 days to add marzipan and icing ◆
◆ **Cooking** 3½–4 hours ◆ **Makes** 23 cm (9 in) round cake ◆

METHOD

Heat the oven to 325°F (170°C/Gas 3) and grease a 23 cm (9 in) round
tin. Line with 3 layers of greaseproof paper, greased on both sides, and
standing up at least 3 cm (1¼ in) above the rim of the tin.

Beat the butter well until soft and fluffy. Add the sugar and beat
thoroughly. In a separate bowl, beat the eggs, treacle, sherry, vanilla
and almond essence together. Then, sift the flours, salt and spices into
another bowl.

With a wooden spoon, mix the beaten eggs and the flour alternately
into the butter and sugar mixture. Mix, but do not beat, to blend well
together. Add the dried fruit and nuts, and stir well to make sure that
the fruit is evenly distributed.

Turn into the prepared tin and level with a palette knife. Bake for 30
minutes and then reduce the heat to 300°F (200°C/Gas 2) and bake for a
further 3–3½ hours. Test by pressing the cake lightly with your finger. If
the cake springs back, it is ready; if not, return it to the oven and cook
for a little longer.

Remove from the oven and leave for 10 minutes in the tin to cool
before turning out on to a wire rack to cool completely. When cold,
wrap well in foil and keep airtight until required.

The marzipan can be added to the cake once it is cold, or, if preferred,
2–3 days before the icing is added. To make the marzipan, mix the icing
sugar and caster sugar (if using) together with the ground almonds. Add
the lemon juice, almond essence and enough egg yolk to give a pliable
but dry paste. Turn on to a sugared board and knead until smooth.

To apply the marzipan, place the Christmas cake on a board or plate.
Roll out the marzipan on a sugared board to a thickness of about ½ cm
(¼ in). Cut out a circle to fit the top of the cake. From the rest of the
marzipan, cut out strips wide enough to cover the sides of the cake.
Heat the jam with the water for the glaze in a saucepan, bring to the
boil and then sieve and reheat. Brush thinly all over the cake, including

the sides. Place the circle of marzipan on top of the cake, and press the strips around. Using your fingers, gradually mould the joins together so that the entire cake is covered in marzipan. Leave in a warm, dry place for 2–3 days to dry out.

The royal icing should be applied to the Christmas cake about 2–3 days before the cake is going to be eaten. To make the icing, put the egg whites in a shallow bowl. Add 30 ml (2 tbsp) of the icing sugar and beat gently together. Gradually add the remaining icing sugar, beating well, until the icing is thick and smooth, and very white. Add the lemon juice and beat again. Add the glycerine and mix in carefully.

To apply the icing to the cake, place the cake on the plate or cake board on which it is to be served, if it is not on it already. Using a palette knife, cover the entire surface of the cake with the icing. For a smooth finish, dip the palette knife in boiling water. For a snow-like effect, pull at the icing with a knife to form peaks. Add holly, robins or whatever decorations you prefer. Store in an airtight container.

For the glaze
30 ml (2 tbsp) apricot jam
10 ml (2 tsp) water

For the royal icing
2 medium egg whites
450 g (1 lb) icing sugar
5 ml (1 tsp) freshly squeezed lemon juice
5 ml (1 tsp) glycerine

◆ CHRISTMAS LOG ◆

This festive log can be decorated with holly leaves, mistletoe, model robins or similar.

◆ **Preparation** 20–25 minutes ◆ **Cooking** 8–10 minutes ◆ **Makes** 18 cm (7 in) log ◆

METHOD

Heat the oven to 425°F (220°C/Gas 7) and grease and line a 28 × 18 cm (11 × 7 in) Swiss roll tin.

Mix together the cocoa, flour, salt and baking powder. Beat the eggs and sugar together in a bowl set over a saucepan of simmering water until very thick and pale. Remove from the heat.

Using a metal spoon, fold in the flour. Spread the mixture into the prepared tin and bake for 8–10 minutes until the sponge springs back when pressed lightly with a finger. Have ready a piece of greaseproof paper sprinkled with caster sugar.

When cooked, remove from the oven and turn on to the sugared paper. Remove the lining paper and roll the sponge up carefully. Hold in place and allow to cool. Unroll and remove the sugared paper.

To make the icing, blend the cocoa with the hot water and leave to cool. Cream the butter with half the icing sugar until light and very fluffy. Add the milk, brandy, cocoa mixture and the rest of the icing sugar and beat hard until well blended and fluffy.

Spread one-third of the icing on the inside of the cake. Roll up the sponge carefully and spread the other two-thirds all over. Use a fork to make bark-like markings on top and sprinkle with a little icing sugar.

INGREDIENTS

For the log
5 ml (1 tsp) margarine, to grease tin
25 g (1 oz) cocoa powder
50 g (2 oz) plain flour, sifted
Pinch of salt
5 ml (1 tsp) baking powder
3 medium eggs, beaten
75 g (3 oz) caster sugar, plus 45 ml (3 tbsp) to sugar paper

For the filling and topping
30 ml (2 tbsp) cocoa powder, plus 15 ml (1 tbsp) to sprinkle log
15 ml (1 tbsp) hot water
75 g (3 oz) butter
275 g (10 oz) icing sugar
37 ml (2½ tbsp) milk
10 ml (2 tsp) brandy

INGREDIENTS

225 g (8 oz) butter, softened,
plus 5 ml (1 tsp) to grease
tin
225 g (8 oz) caster sugar
Grated rind of 1 large orange
4 medium eggs, beaten
225 g (8 oz) plain flour, sifted
50 g (2 oz) ground almonds
25 g (1 oz) mixed candied peel
100 g (4 oz) currants
100 g (4 oz) sultanas
100 g (4 oz) raisins
50 g (2 oz) glacé cherries,
quartered
40–50 split almonds

◆ DUNDEE CAKE ◆

*This traditional Scottish fruit cake is always popular with its light
texture and almond flavour.*

◆ **Preparation** 15 minutes ◆ **Cooking** 2½–3 hours ◆
◆ **Makes** 18 cm (7 in) round cake or 900 g (2 lb) loaf ◆

METHOD

Heat the oven to 300°F (150°C/Gas 2) and grease and line an 18 cm
(7 in) round tin or a 900 g (2 lb) loaf tin.

Cream the butter and sugar together until light and fluffy. Beat in the
orange rind and the eggs, one at a time, adding 15 ml (1 tbsp) of the
flour with each egg. Beat thoroughly.

With a metal spoon, stir in the ground almonds and dried fruit. Fold
in the remaining flour carefully. Turn the mixture into the prepared tin
and arrange the split almonds over the entire top.

Bake the cake for 2½–3 hours until a skewer comes out clean.
Remove from the oven and leave in the tin for 2–3 minutes before
turning out on to a wire rack to cool completely.

INGREDIENTS

225 g (8 oz) self-raising flour,
sifted
½ tsp baking powder
7.5 ml (1½ tsp) ground mixed
spice
7.5 ml (1½ tsp) ground
nutmeg
100 g (4 oz) butter or
margarine, softened, plus
5 ml (1 tsp) to grease tin
175 g (6 oz) soft brown sugar
10 ml (2 tsp) syrup
2 medium eggs, beaten
450 g (1 lb) mixed dried fruit
(raisins, currants, sultanas,
candied peel and cherries)
30 ml (2 tbsp) warm milk

◆ FAMILY FRUIT CAKE ◆

*This is a good everyday cake, moist and spicy. More spices can be added
if desired.*

◆ **Preparation** 20 minutes ◆ **Cooking** 1¾–2 hours ◆ **Makes** 18 cm (7 in) round cake ◆

METHOD

Heat the oven to 325°F (170°C/Gas 3) and grease and line an 18 cm
(7 in) round tin.

Mix the flour, baking powder and spices together. In a separate bowl,
cream the fat and sugar together until light and fluffy. Add the syrup
and beat well. Beat in the eggs, a little at a time, adding 15 ml (1 tbsp) of
flour between each addition. Beat hard to incorporate plenty of air.

Mix in the rest of the flour with a wooden spoon, add the dried fruit
and mix well. Add the warm milk and beat until the mixture is moist
and well blended.

Pour into the prepared tin and bake for 1¾–2 hours until a skewer
comes out clean. Remove from the oven and turn out on to a wire
rack to cool.

◆ GINGER CAKE ◆

This is a deliciously sticky gingerbread to which you can add almost any dried fruit instead of, or as well as, the crystallized ginger. It is excellent with raisins, sultanas, chopped dates or candied peel, or with a mixture of any of these.

◆ **Preparation** 10 minutes ◆ **Cooking** 1 hour ◆
◆ **Makes** 18 cm (7 in) round cake or 900 g (2 lb) loaf ◆

METHOD

Heat the oven to 350°F (180°C/Gas 4) and grease and line an 18 cm (7 in) round tin or a 900 g (2 lb) loaf tin.

In a medium saucepan, melt the fats, syrup and sugar together over a gentle heat until the sugar is dissolved. Do not boil. Remove from the heat and gradually add the flour, salt and spices, beating hard with a wooden spoon. Add the chopped ginger and stir well.

Dissolve the soda in the warm milk. Pour into the cake mixture and mix carefully until well blended.

Pour the mixture into the prepared tin and bake for 1 hour until brown and firm, and a skewer comes out clean. Remove from the oven and leave to cool in the tin for 10–15 minutes before turning out on to a wire rack to cool completely.

INGREDIENTS

50 g (2 oz) margarine or butter, plus 5 ml (1 tsp) to grease tin
50 g (2 oz) lard
50 g (2 oz) demerara sugar
60 ml (4 tbsp) syrup
250 g (9 oz) self-raising flour, sifted
Pinch of salt
15 ml (1 tbsp) ground ginger
10 ml (2 tsp) ground mixed spice
100 g (4 oz) crystallized ginger, chopped finely, or any dried fruit of choice
$\frac{1}{2}$ tsp bicarbonate of soda
150 ml ($\frac{1}{4}$ pt) warm milk

◆ MADEIRA CAKE ◆

A light sponge cake with a subtle lemon flavour, traditionally served at tea time.

◆ **Preparation** 10 minutes ◆ **Cooking** 1½ hours ◆ **Makes** 18 cm (7 in) round cake ◆

METHOD

Heat the oven to 350°F (180°C/Gas 4) and grease and line an 18 cm (7 in) round tin.

Mix together the flour and baking powder. In a separate bowl, cream the fat, sugar and lemon rind together until light and fluffy. Beat in the eggs, a little at a time, adding 15 ml (1 tbsp) of the flour with each addition. Beat hard to incorporate plenty of air.

Using a metal spoon, fold in the remaining flour and then add the milk. Mix together thoroughly and pour into the prepared tin.

Bake the cake for 1 hour. Take out of the oven, press the strips of citrus peel lightly over the top of the cake and bake for a further 30 minutes until golden and well risen, and a skewer comes out clean. Remove from the oven and leave to cool in the tin for at least 5 minutes before turning out on to a wire rack to cool completely.

INGREDIENTS

225 g (8 oz) plain flour, sifted
5 ml (1 tsp) baking powder
175 g (6 oz) butter or margarine, softened, plus 5 ml (1 tsp) to grease tin
175 g (6 oz) caster sugar
Grated rind of $\frac{1}{2}$ lemon
3 medium eggs, beaten
30 ml (2 tbsp) milk, at room temperature
2–3 thin slices of candied citrus peel

Pictured opposite page 97

INGREDIENTS

For the cake
225 g (8 oz) plain flour, sifted
10 ml (2 tsp) baking powder
½ tsp bicarbonate of soda
5 ml (1 tsp) ground mixed
   spice
175 g (6 oz) caster sugar
150 ml (¼ pt) milk, at room
   temperature
100 g (4 oz) butter, softened,
   plus 5 ml (1 tsp) to grease
   tin
Grated rind of 1 lemon
2 medium eggs, beaten
100 g (4 oz) mincemeat

For the topping
50 g (2 oz) butter, softened
175 g (6 oz) icing sugar
15 ml (1 tbsp) brandy
Brazil nuts, to decorate

Pictured opposite page 81

MINCEMEAT CAKE WITH ♦ BRANDY BUTTER TOPPING ♦

This moist and spicy cake can be made with bought mincemeat or the home-made variety on page 134.

♦ **Preparation** 15 minutes ♦ **Cooking** 1 hour ♦ **Makes** 18 cm (7 in) square cake ♦

METHOD

Heat the oven to 325°F (170°C/Gas 3) and grease and line an 18 cm (7 in) square tin.

Mix together the flour, baking powder, soda and spice. Add the sugar, milk, butter and lemon rind and beat until smooth. Gradually add the eggs and beat thoroughly. Add the mincemeat and stir in well.

Pour into the prepared tin and bake for 1 hour until firm. Remove from the oven and leave to cool in the tin for 5 minutes before turning out on to a wire rack to cool completely.

Cream the butter and icing sugar together until light and fluffy, and then beat in the brandy. Spread on to the cake and swirl a knife blade through the icing to create a pattern. Decorate with the brazil nuts.

INGREDIENTS

For the cake
100 g (4 oz) plain chocolate
150 g (5 oz) margarine or
   butter, softened, plus 10 ml
   (2 tsp) to grease tins
150 g (5 oz) caster sugar
3 medium eggs, beaten
15 ml (1 tbsp) milk
225 g (8 oz) self-raising flour,
   sifted
Pinch of salt

For the filling
30 g (1½ oz) butter, softened
100 g (4 oz) icing sugar, plus
   30 ml (2 tbsp) to dredge
   cake
10 ml (2 tsp) milk
15 ml (1 tbsp) cocoa powder
15 ml (1 tbsp) hot water

♦ MOIST CHOCOLATE CAKE ♦

If preferred, the chocolate icing on this cake can be substituted with vanilla icing. Use ¼ tsp vanilla essence instead of the cocoa.

♦ **Preparation** 15 minutes ♦ **Cooking** 35–40 minutes ♦ **Makes** 18 cm (7 in) round cake ♦

METHOD

Heat the oven to 350°F (180°C/Gas 4) and grease and line 2 × 18 cm (7 in) round sandwich tins.

Melt the chocolate in a bowl set over a pan of simmering water.

Cream the fat and sugar together until light and fluffy. Beat in the eggs, one at a time. Stir the milk into the melted chocolate and add to the mixture. Beat thoroughly. Using a metal spoon, fold in the flour and salt and mix well.

Pour into the prepared tins and bake for 35–40 minutes until firm and well risen. Remove from the oven and cool in the tins for 15 minutes before turning out on to a wire rack to cool completely.

For the filling, cream the butter and icing sugar together. Add the rest of the ingredients and beat well. When the cakes are cold, sandwich them together with the icing. Dredge the top with the extra icing sugar.

MRS PETTIGREW'S FAMOUS
♦ LEMON CAKE ♦

*This cake should be really lemony and moist, so if the lemons you buy
are not very juicy use an extra one or add a little bottled lemon juice.*

♦ **Preparation** 10 minutes ♦ **Cooking** 1 hour ♦
♦ **Makes** 18 cm (7 in) round cake or 900 g (2 lb) loaf ♦

METHOD

Heat the oven to 325°F (170°C/Gas 3) and grease and line an 18 cm
(7 in) round tin or a 900 g (2 lb) loaf tin.

Grate 2 of the lemons and juice all 3. Put the lemon juice in a bowl
with the 45 ml (3 tbsp) sugar for the topping and stand in a warm place
until needed. The top of the oven is ideal. The sugar should dissolve and
form a syrup with the juice.

Cream the fat and sugar together until very light and fluffy. Add the
eggs, a little at a time, beating thoroughly between each addition. Add
the grated lemon rind and the flour and beat hard. Finally, add the milk
and beat again.

Pour into the prepared tin and bake for 1 hour until golden and well
risen. Remove from the oven and immediately prick the top in 3–4
places. Pour the lemon juice and sugar syrup at once all over the cake so
that the entire top is covered.

Leave the cake in the tin until quite cold, so that all the juice will be
absorbed by the sponge. Then, turn out and wrap the cake in foil until
needed, to keep it fresh.

INGREDIENTS

3 lemons
45 ml (3 tbsp) caster sugar, for
  the topping
100 g (4 oz) margarine or
  butter, softened, plus 5 ml
  (1 tsp) to grease tin
175 g (6 oz) caster sugar
2 large eggs, beaten
175 g (6 oz) self-raising flour,
  sifted
90 ml (3½ fl oz) milk, at room
  temperature

OLD ENGLISH CIDER CAKE
WITH CREAM CHEESE &
♦ GINGER TOPPING ♦

*This moist, apple-flavoured cake can be made without the topping,
if preferred.*

♦ **Preparation** 10 minutes ♦ **Cooking** 40–45 minutes ♦ **Makes** 900 g (2 lb) loaf ♦

METHOD

Heat the oven to 375°F (190°C/Gas 5) and grease and line a 900 g
(2 lb) loaf tin.

Cream the fat and sugar together until light and fluffy. Gradually beat
in the eggs, beating hard between each addition. With a metal spoon,

INGREDIENTS

For the cake
100 g (4 oz) butter or
  margarine, softened, plus
  5 ml (1 tsp) to grease tin
100 g (4 oz) soft brown sugar
2 medium eggs, beaten
225 g (8 oz) plain flour, sifted
5 ml (1 tsp) baking powder
5 ml (1 tsp) ground nutmeg
½ tsp ground ginger
150 ml (¼ pt) medium-dry
  cider

Continued overleaf

For the topping
100 g (4 oz) cream cheese,
    softened
100 g (4 oz) icing sugar
5 ml (1 tsp) ground ginger
25 g (1 oz) crystallized ginger,
    chopped finely

Pictured opposite page 97

INGREDIENTS
½ quantity shortcrust pastry,
    using 100 g (4 oz) flour (see
    page 139)
5 ml (1 tsp) margarine, to
    grease plate
50–75 g (2–3 oz) flour, to
    flour board
15–30 ml (1–2 tbsp) milk
225 g (8 oz) mincemeat

Pictured opposite page 81

fold in the flour, baking powder, nutmeg and ginger and mix well.
Lastly, stir in the cider.

Pour into the prepared tin and bake for 40–45 minutes until light
golden and firm. Remove from the oven and turn out on to a wire
rack to cool.

For the topping, beat all the ingredients together until very smooth.
Spread over the top of the cake. Draw the prongs of a fork through the
topping to make a pattern.

OPEN MINCEMEAT
◆ TART ◆

*This lattice-topped tart is traditionally for Christmas but is popular all
year round. Use bought mincemeat or the home-made variety on
page 134.*

◆ **Preparation** 20–25 minutes, plus 20 minutes for pastry ◆ **Cooking** 25–30 minutes ◆
◆ **Makes** 20 cm (8 in) tart ◆

METHOD
Make the pastry as on page 139 and chill for 15 minutes.

Heat the oven to 450°F (230°C/Gas 8) and grease a 20 cm (8 in)
ovenproof plate.

Roll out the pastry on a floured board to a thickness of about 5 mm
(¼ in). Lay the pastry carefully over the greased plate and, using a sharp
knife, trim off the excess. Cut out some strips, about 2.5 cm (1 in) wide,
from this excess pastry. Brush one side of each strip with milk and then
lay them, milky side down, around the edge of the pastry circle to form
a 'wall'. Press the strips down firmly, brushing a little more milk on to
the edges of the strips where they join. This 'wall' is to stop the
mincemeat from running out during cooking.

Using a blunt knife or the prongs of a fork, mark a pattern all around
the pastry over the strips so that the tart will have a decorative edge.
Spoon the mincemeat into the middle of the pastry and spread it out to
cover the base.

Roll out the remaining pieces of pastry into sausage shapes, about
1 cm (½ in) in diameter and 15–18 cm (6–7 in) long. Use a little milk to
bind the pieces of pastry together if necessary. Lay these strips in a lattice
pattern over the top of the tart, trimming to fit the inside edge of the
tart where necessary.

Bake for 15 minutes and then lower the oven temperature to 400°F
(200°C/Gas 6) and cook for a further 10–15 minutes. The pastry should
be golden. Take out and serve hot or cold.

◆ POUND CAKE ◆

Traditional recipes for Pound cake vary, but this modern version gives a good fruity, moist cake with the extra flavour of brandy or sherry.

◆ **Preparation** 30 minutes ◆ **Cooking** 2–2½ hours ◆ **Makes** 23 cm (9 in) round cake ◆

INGREDIENTS

450 g (1 lb) plain flour, sifted
10 ml (2 tsp) baking powder
225 g (8 oz) butter, softened, plus 10 ml (2 tsp) to grease tin
225 g (8 oz) caster sugar
4 medium eggs
Grated rind of 1 lemon
50 g (2 oz) mixed candied peel
225 g (8 oz) currants
50 g (2 oz) finely chopped blanched almonds
50 ml (2 fl oz) brandy or sherry

METHOD

Heat the oven to 325°F (170°C/Gas 3) and grease and line a 23 cm (9 in) round tin.

Mix together the flour and baking powder. In a separate bowl, cream the butter and sugar together until light and fluffy. Add the eggs, one at a time, beating well and adding 15 ml (1 tbsp) of the flour with each egg. Add the lemon rind and beat the mixture thoroughly.

With a metal spoon, fold in the rest of the flour and the candied peel, currants and chopped almonds. Mix thoroughly to make sure that all the ingredients are evenly distributed. Lastly, stir the brandy or sherry into the mixture.

Turn into the prepared tin and bake for 2–2½ hours until a skewer comes out clean. Remove from the oven and turn out on to a wire rack to cool.

◆ SEED CAKE ◆

Seed cake is basically a Madeira cake with the added flavour and texture of caraway seeds.

◆ **Preparation** 10 minutes ◆ **Cooking** 1–1¼ hours ◆
◆ **Makes** 18 cm (7 in) round cake or 900 g (2 lb) loaf ◆

INGREDIENTS

175 g (6 oz) butter or margarine, softened, plus 5 ml (1 tsp) to grease tin
175 g (6 oz) caster sugar
3 medium eggs
225 g (8 oz) plain flour, sifted
10 ml (2 tsp) baking powder
Pinch of salt
Pinch of bicarbonate of soda
25 g (1 oz) caraway seeds
½ tsp ground cinnamon
15 ml (1 tbsp) milk, at room temperature

METHOD

Heat the oven to 350°F (180°C/Gas 4) and grease and line an 18 cm (7 in) round tin or a 900 g (2 lb) loaf tin.

Cream the fat and sugar together until light and fluffy. Place the eggs in a bowl set over a saucepan of simmering water, and beat until pale and thick. Beat the eggs into the fat and sugar mixture.

Mix together all the dry ingredients and fold into the mixture with a wooden spoon. Add the milk and mix well.

Pour into the prepared tin and bake for 1–1¼ hours until golden and firm. Remove from the oven and leave to cool in the tin for 15 minutes before turning out on to a wire rack to cool completely.

INGREDIENTS

225 g (8 oz) marzipan, bought
  or made with $\frac{1}{3}$ quantity of
  recipe on page 72
225 g (8 oz) plain flour, sifted
5 ml (1 tsp) baking powder
Pinch of salt
5 ml (1 tsp) ground mixed
  spice
Large pinch of ground mace
175 g (6 oz) butter, softened,
  plus 5 ml (1 tsp) to grease
  tin
175 g (6 oz) soft brown sugar
3 medium eggs
30 ml (2 tbsp) milk
100 g (4 oz) raisins
175 g (6 oz) currants
50 g (2 oz) sultanas
50 g (2 oz) mixed candied peel
50 g (2 oz) glacé cherries,
  rinsed, dried and quartered
Beaten egg white, to glaze
  cake
Wide yellow ribbon, to
  decorate cake

Pictured opposite

♦ SIMNEL CAKE ♦

This cake was traditionally made during Lent for Mothering Sunday. Girls in service used to be given a holiday to visit their parents, and they would take a Simnel Cake as a present for their mothers. The 11 marzipan balls represent the apostles, excepting Judas.

♦ **Preparation** 35–40 minutes ♦ **Cooking** 1½ hours ♦ **Makes** 15 cm (6 in) round cake ♦

METHOD

Heat the oven to 350°F (180°C/Gas 4) and grease and line a 15 cm (6 in) round tin. Roll out a third of the marzipan into a circle slightly smaller than the tin.

Mix together the flour, baking powder, salt, spice and mace in a bowl. In a separate bowl, cream the butter and sugar together until light and fluffy. Beat in the eggs, one at a time, adding 15 ml (1 tbsp) of the flour with each egg. Beat the mixture thoroughly after each addition.

Using a metal spoon, fold in the rest of the flour a little at a time, alternating with the milk. Fold in the fruit. Pour half the mixture into the prepared tin and smooth with a palette knife. Lay the circle of marzipan on top. Pour in the rest of the cake mixture.

Bake the cake for 30 minutes and then reduce the heat to 300°F (150°C/Gas 2) and cook for a further hour until a skewer comes out clean. Remove from the oven and leave to cool in the tin for 10 minutes before carefully turning out the cake on to a wire rack to cool completely.

Divide the remaining marzipan into 2 halves. Break one half into 11 pieces and roll each in your palm to form balls. Roll out the other half into a circle to fit the top of the cake.

Brush the top of the cake with egg white and place the marzipan circle on top. Brush a little more egg white on to the bottom of each ball and place around the edge of the cake.

Tie a yellow ribbon around the outside of the cake and secure it carefully with 2 pins.

Family & seasonal cakes Clockwise from left: Simnel cake (see page 80); Chocolate cinnamon roll (see page 71); Banana & cherry cake (see page 71).

♦ SPECIAL CHOCOLATE CAKE ♦

This cake is made with oil and becomes moister the longer you keep it.

♦ **Preparation** 10 minutes ♦ **Cooking** 40–45 minutes ♦ **Makes** 18 cm (7 in) round cake ♦

METHOD

Heat the oven to 325°F (170°C/Gas 3) and oil and line 2 × 18 cm (7 in) round sandwich tins.

Mix the flour, baking powder, cocoa, soda and sugar together. In a separate bowl, beat the treacle, eggs, oil and milk together. Pour this on to the flour mixture and stir carefully until well blended. Beat well.

Pour the mixture into the prepared tins and bake for 40–45 minutes until the cake springs back when pressed lightly with a finger. Remove from the oven and leave in the tins for 2–3 minutes to cool slightly before turning out on to a wire rack to cool completely.

For the filling, cream the icing sugar and butter together until very smooth and fluffy. Beat in the cocoa and hot water and blend thoroughly. Spread the filling on to one of the cakes and place the other cake carefully on top. Dredge the top of the cake with caster sugar.

INGREDIENTS

For the cake
175 g (6 oz) plain flour, sifted
5 ml (1 tsp) baking powder
30 ml (2 tbsp) cocoa powder
5 ml (1 tsp) bicarbonate of soda
150 g (5 oz) caster sugar
30 ml (2 tbsp) black treacle
2 medium eggs, beaten
150 ml ($\frac{1}{4}$ pt) vegetable oil
150 ml ($\frac{1}{4}$ pt) warm milk

For the filling
175 g (6 oz) icing sugar
50 g (2 oz) butter, softened
25 g (1 oz) cocoa powder
30 ml (2 tbsp) hot water

Pictured opposite page 65

♦ SWISS ROLL ♦

Any jam can be used for the filling, or try butter icing or fresh cream.

♦ **Preparation** 15 minutes ♦ **Cooking** 7–10 minutes ♦ **Makes** 18 cm (7 in) roll ♦

METHOD

Heat the oven to 400°F (200°C/Gas 6) and grease and line a 28 × 18 cm (11 × 7 in) Swiss roll tin.

Beat the eggs and sugar together in a bowl set over a saucepan of simmering water until the mixture leaves a trail when the beater is lifted. This will take 7–8 minutes. Fold in the flour and hot water.

Pour into the prepared tin and bake for 8–10 minutes until light golden and firm. Have ready a sheet of greaseproof paper. Place it on top of a damp cloth and sprinkle with 30 ml (2 tbsp) of sugar. Remove the cake from the oven and turn immediately on to the sugared paper. Peel off the lining paper.

While still hot, trim the edges of the cake and spread it with the raspberry jam, covering all the sponge except for 1.5 cm ($\frac{1}{2}$ in) at one end. Roll the cake up towards that end and hold in place for a few minutes. Transfer carefully to a wire rack to cool. Before serving, dredge with 30 ml (2 tbsp) caster sugar.

INGREDIENTS

5 ml (1 tsp) margarine, to grease tin
3 medium eggs
100 g (4 oz) caster sugar, plus 60 ml (4 tbsp) to sugar paper and dredge roll
75 g (3 oz) plain flour, sifted
15 ml (1 tbsp) hot water
45 ml (3 tbsp) raspberry jam

Christmas tea Clockwise from top: Mincemeat cake with brandy butter topping (see page 76); Open mincemeat tart (see page 78); Christmas cake (see page 72); Brandy snaps (see page 60).

INGREDIENTS

100 g (4 oz) margarine or
  butter, softened, plus 5 ml
  (1 tsp) to grease tins
100 g (4 oz) caster sugar, plus
  15 ml (1 tbsp) to dredge
  cake
2 medium eggs, beaten
100 g (4 oz) self-raising flour,
  sifted
15 ml (1 tbsp) boiling water
50–75 g (2–3 oz) raspberry
  jam

Pictured opposite page 129

♦ VICTORIA SPONGE ♦

*Although raspberry jam is the traditional filling for this cake, it is
delicious with any type of filling. Try vanilla or chocolate butter icing,
or use jam or fresh fruit with whipped cream.*

♦ **Preparation** 10 minutes ♦ **Cooking** 20–25 minutes ♦ **Makes** 18 cm (7 in) round cake ♦

METHOD

Heat the oven to 350°F (180°C/Gas 4) and grease and line 2 × 18 cm
(7 in) round sandwich tins.

Cream the fat and sugar together until light and fluffy. Beat in the
eggs, a little at a time, and adding 15 ml (1 tbsp) of the flour between
each addition. Beat very thoroughly. Fold in the remaining flour with a
metal spoon. Finally, stir in the boiling water and mix well.

Divide the mixture between the prepared tins and bake for 20–25
minutes until the cake is lightly browned and springs back when pressed
lightly with a finger.

Remove from the oven and turn out on to a wire rack to cool. When
cold, spread the underside of one cake with jam, lay the other cake
carefully on top and dredge with the extra caster sugar.

INGREDIENTS

175 g (6 oz) butter, softened,
  plus 5 ml (1 tsp) to grease
  tin
350 g (12 oz) plain flour, sifted
100 g (4 oz) soft brown sugar
15 g ($\frac{1}{2}$ oz) ground cinnamon
5 ml (1 tsp) grated nutmeg
100 g (4 oz) raisins
100 g (4 oz) currants
100 g (4 oz) mixed candied
  peel
50 g (2 oz) chopped almonds
3 medium eggs
50 ml (2 fl oz) brandy
About 30 ml (2 tbsp) single
  cream

♦ WHITBY YULE CAKE ♦

*This cake was traditionally offered with a glass of cherry brandy to
visitors between Christmas Day and New Year's Day.*

♦ **Preparation** 10–15 minutes ♦ **Cooking** $2\frac{1}{2}$–3 hours ♦ **Makes** 9 pieces ♦

METHOD

Heat the oven to 325°F (170°C/Gas 3) and grease and line a 20 cm
(8 in) square tin.

Rub or cut the butter into the flour until the mixture resembles fine
breadcrumbs. Mix in the dry ingredients.

Beat the eggs with the brandy. Add to the dry ingredients and mix
well with a fork. Add enough of the cream to mix to a soft dough. Press
into the prepared tin and mark into 9 squares, cutting half-way through
the dough.

Bake the cake for $2\frac{1}{2}$–3 hours. Remove from the oven and turn out
on to a wire rack to cool. When cold, break into rough pieces along the
marked lines.

FANCY & PARTY CAKES

Several of the cakes in this section are also suitable for dinner parties, for instance the Raspberry gâteau, the Strawberry shortcake and the Walnut and lemon meringue cake. All make excellent desserts. I have included them in this chapter because an elaborate sweet of this kind provides a stunning centrepiece at a tea table and makes guests feel that a real effort has been made to provide something special.

Cakes can be served on pretty china or glass plates and stands. A range of cake stands are available, some large enough to stand on the floor. These may be covered with linen cloths or paper doilies. There are also smaller 2- or 3-tier stands made for the table, and a special gâteau can be placed on a single-tiered stand.

♦ ALMOND CHERRY CAKE ♦

Cherries always tend to sink to the bottom of cakes, so do not worry if this happens. This cake is delicious and moist, and will keep well for up to 10 days if stored in an airtight container.

♦ **Preparation** 25 minutes ♦ **Cooking** 50–55 minutes ♦ **Makes** 18 cm (7 in) round cake ♦

METHOD

Heat the oven to 350°F (180°C/Gas 4) and grease and line an 18 cm (7 in) round tin.

Cream the butter and sugar together until light and fluffy. Add the eggs, one at a time, gradually mixing in the ground almonds and beating thoroughly between each addition. Using a metal spoon, fold in the flour, cherries and almond essence and mix well.

Pour into the prepared tin and bake for 50–55 minutes until a skewer comes out clean. Remove from the oven and leave to cool in the tin for

INGREDIENTS

For the cake
100 g (4 oz) butter, softened, plus 5 ml (1 tsp) to grease tin
150 g (5 oz) caster sugar
3 large eggs
90 g (3½ oz) ground almonds
40 g (1½ oz) self-raising flour, sifted
175 g (6 oz) dark glacé cherries
5 ml (1 tsp) almond essence

Continued overleaf

For the topping
50 g (2 oz) butter, softened
100 g (4 oz) icing sugar
5 ml (1 tsp) amaretto
4 glacé cherries, halved
8 split almonds

INGREDIENTS

100 g (4 oz) margarine or
    butter, plus 5 ml (1 tsp) to
    grease tin
150 g (5 oz) caster sugar, plus
    30 ml (2 tbsp) to dust cake
6 medium eggs, separated
$\frac{1}{4}$ tsp vanilla essence
45–60 ml (3–4 tbsp) ground
    semolina, plus 15–30 ml
    (1–2 tbsp) extra if necessary
500 g (1 lb 2 oz) curd cheese
Juice of $\frac{1}{2}$ lemon
$\frac{1}{4}$ tsp baking powder
225 g (8 oz) raisins

Pictured opposite page 112

INGREDIENTS

For the cake
175 g (6 oz) self-raising flour,
    sifted
Pinch of salt
5 ml (1 tsp) baking powder
150 g (5 oz) butter, softened,
    plus 10 ml (2 tsp) to grease
150 g (5 oz) caster sugar
3 medium eggs
25 ml (5 tsp) instant coffee
15 ml (1 tbsp) boiling water
75 g (3 oz) chopped walnuts

15 minutes before turning the cake out carefully on to a wire rack to cool completely.

For the topping, beat all the ingredients together until very fluffy and smooth. Spread on the top of the cake and make a pattern with a fork or with the edge of a round-bladed knife. Lay the cherry halves and nuts alternately around the edge of the cake, also laying a few in the middle.

◆ BAKED CHEESECAKE ◆

Cheesecakes have been popular in England for at least 700 years. This traditional version is more substantial than the modern light, fluffy cheesecakes, and has the added texture and sweetness of raisins.

◆ **Preparation** 20–25 minutes ◆ **Cooking** $1\frac{1}{2}$–$1\frac{3}{4}$ hours ◆ **Makes** 20 cm (8 in) round cake ◆

METHOD

Heat the oven to 350°F (180°C/Gas 4) and grease and line a 20 cm (8 in) round tin.

Cream the fat, sugar and egg yolks together until light and fluffy. Add the vanilla and beat again. Very gradually add the semolina and cheese, beating well after each addition. If the mixture is rather wet, add the extra semolina.

Add the lemon juice, baking powder and raisins and mix well. Beat the egg whites until stiff and fold carefully into the mixture.

Pour into the prepared tin and bake for $1\frac{1}{4}$ hours until golden. Do not open the oven door during this time. Switch off the oven and leave the cake to finish cooking, about 15–30 minutes, until golden.

Remove the cheesecake from the oven and leave to cool completely in the tin. Turn out on to a serving dish and dust with caster sugar.

◆ COFFEE & WALNUT CAKE ◆

This attractive cake is always very popular. The strength of the coffee flavouring can be varied to suit personal taste.

◆ **Preparation** 20 minutes ◆ **Cooking** 35–40 minutes ◆ **Makes** 18 cm (7 in) round cake ◆

METHOD

Heat the oven to 350°F (180°C/Gas 4) and grease and line 2 × 18 cm (7 in) round sandwich tins.

Mix together the flour, salt and baking powder. In a separate bowl, cream the butter and sugar together until light and fluffy. Add the eggs, one at a time, mixing in 15 ml (1 tbsp) of flour between each egg, and beating thoroughly with each addition.

Mix in the rest of the flour and beat again. Dissolve the coffee in the boiling water and stir into the mixture with the walnuts. Mix until well blended.

Spoon into the prepared tins and bake for 35–40 minutes until firm. Remove from the oven and turn out the cakes immediately on to a wire rack to cool.

For the filling and topping, cream the icing sugar, butter, coffee and water together, adding more icing sugar if the mixture is too soft and runny. It needs to be fairly stiff. Use the icing to sandwich the cakes together and to cover the top and sides. Swirl the icing with a warm knife blade to make a pattern and decorate with the walnut halves.

For the filling and topping
About 350 g (12 oz) icing
 sugar
225 g (8 oz) butter, softened
20 ml (4 tsp) instant coffee
5 ml (1 tsp) water
9–10 walnut halves

Pictured opposite page 112

ORANGE CHOCOLATE
♦ CAKE ♦

This is a lovely soft sponge cake with the excellent combination of chocolate and orange.

♦ **Preparation** 20 minutes ♦ **Cooking** 40–45 minutes ♦ **Makes** 18 cm (7 in) round cake ♦

METHOD

Heat the oven to 350°F (180°C/Gas 4) and grease and line an 18 cm (7 in) round tin.

Dissolve the cocoa in the water. Cream the fat and sugar together until light and fluffy. Beat in the eggs, one at a time, beating hard between each addition. Add the cocoa mixture and beat thoroughly. Using a metal spoon, fold in the flour. Add the orange rind and juice and mix well so that all the ingredients are evenly distributed.

Turn into the prepared tin and bake for 40–45 minutes until firm. Remove from the oven and leave to cool in the tin for 10–15 minutes before turning out on to a wire rack to cool completely.

For the filling, cream the butter and icing sugar together until soft and fluffy. Gradually beat in the orange rind and juice, and then beat hard until soft and smooth.

When the cake is quite cold, cut in half horizontally and use half the filling to sandwich the cake halves together. Use the remaining filling to ice the top, swirling it with a warm knife blade to make a pattern. Decorate with the fresh orange segments and serve immediately.

INGREDIENTS

For the cake
30 ml (2 tbsp) cocoa powder
30 ml (2 tbsp) warm water
100 g (4 oz) margarine or
 butter, softened, plus 5 ml
 (1 tsp) to grease tin
150 g (5 oz) caster sugar
2 large eggs, beaten
100 g (4 oz) self-raising flour,
 sifted
Grated rind of 1 large orange
30 ml (2 tbsp) freshly
 squeezed orange juice

For the filling and topping
225 g (8 oz) unsalted butter,
 softened
225 g (8 oz) icing sugar
Grated rind and juice of ½
 orange
10–12 fresh orange segments,
 skinned and seeded

INGREDIENTS

For the cake
5 ml (1 tsp) margarine, to
  grease tin
3 medium eggs, separated
75 g (3 oz) caster sugar
Grated rind of ½ lemon
50 g (2 oz) plain flour, sifted
15 g (½ oz) ground almonds

For the filling and topping
450 g (1 lb) fresh or frozen
  raspberries, hulled
30 ml (2 tbsp) caster sugar
275 ml (½ pt) double cream

♦ RASPBERRY GÂTEAU ♦

This gâteau can also be made with strawberries, if desired.

♦ **Preparation** 30 minutes ♦ **Cooking** 35–40 minutes ♦ **Makes** 23 cm (9 in) round cake ♦

METHOD

Heat the oven to 350°F (180°C/Gas 4) and grease and line a 23 cm (9 in) round tin.

Beat the egg yolks and sugar together until thick and creamy. Add the lemon rind and continue beating until the mixture leaves a trail when the beater is lifted.

Using a metal spoon, fold in the flour and almonds. Beat the egg whites until stiff and fold into the mixture with a metal spoon.

Pour into the prepared tin and bake for 35–40 minutes until well risen and golden. Remove from the oven and turn out immediately on to a wire rack to cool. When cold, cut in half horizontally.

Reserve 16–18 of the best raspberries for decoration. Lay the remainder across one half of the cake, and sprinkle with half the sugar. Sandwich with the other half of cake.

Just before serving, whip the cream until stiff. Spread all over the top and sides of the cake. Arrange the rest of the raspberries over the top and sprinkle with the remaining sugar.

INGREDIENTS

For the cake
2 medium eggs
175 g (6 oz) granulated sugar
150 ml (¼ pt) corn oil, plus
  15 ml (1 tbsp) to grease tin
50 g (2 oz) finely chopped
  walnuts
100 g (4 oz) plain flour, sifted
225 g (8 oz) carrots, grated
5 ml (1 tsp) ground cinnamon
5 ml (1 tsp) bicarbonate of
  soda

For the topping
175 g (6 oz) icing sugar
50 g (2 oz) butter, softened
75 g (3 oz) cream cheese
½ tsp vanilla essence

RICH CARROT CAKE
♦ WITH CREAM CHEESE ♦

Carrots make deliciously sweet cakes, and the addition of oil makes this a moist cake that improves with keeping.

♦ **Preparation** 15 minutes ♦ **Cooking** 45–50 minutes ♦ **Makes** 18 cm (7 in) round cake ♦

METHOD

Heat the oven to 375°F (190°C/Gas 5) and oil and line an 18 cm (7 in) round tin.

Beat the eggs and sugar together until thick and very pale. Beat in the oil gradually, and then fold in the rest of the cake ingredients with a metal spoon. Mix well so that all the ingredients are evenly distributed.

Pour into the prepared tin and bake for 45–50 minutes until firm and a skewer comes out clean. Remove from the oven and leave to cool in the tin for 10–15 minutes before turning out on to a wire rack.

For the topping, beat all the ingredients together until very smooth and fluffy. Spread over the top of the cake and use the prongs of a fork to make a pattern.

♦ STRAWBERRY SHORTCAKE ♦

Fresh raspberries can be used instead of strawberries in this shortcake if liked. It is perfect for tea time, and is also a wonderful summertime dessert.

♦ **Preparation** 20 minutes ♦ **Cooking** 20–25 minutes ♦ **Makes** 20 cm (8 in) round cake ♦

METHOD

Heat the oven to 375°F (190°C/Gas 5) and grease and line 2 × 20 cm (8 in) round sandwich tins.

Mix together the flour, baking powder and salt. Rub or cut in the butter until the mixture resembles breadcrumbs. Stir in 100 g (4 oz) of the sugar. Add the egg and mix well with a fork. Add enough of the milk to form a soft dough and knead lightly in the bowl until smooth.

Press into the prepared tins and smooth with a palette knife. Bake for 20–25 minutes until firm and pale golden. Remove from the oven and turn out on to a wire rack to cool.

Put the best 5–6 strawberries aside for decoration. Slice the rest, put them in a bowl and sprinkle with the remaining sugar.

Whip the cream until stiff. Spread a quarter of the cream on to the underside of each shortbread layer. Place the sliced strawberries over one layer of shortbread and place the other layer, cream side down, on top. Spread the rest of the cream over the top of the cake. Cut the remaining strawberries in half and use to decorate.

INGREDIENTS

For the shortcake
225 g (8 oz) self-raising flour, sifted
½ tsp baking powder
Good pinch of salt
75 g (3 oz) butter, softened, plus 10 ml (2 tsp) to grease tins
150 g (5 oz) caster sugar
1 medium egg, beaten
45–60 ml (3–4 tbsp) milk

For the filling and topping
225 g (8 oz) strawberries, hulled
275 ml (½ pt) double cream

Pictured opposite page 112

WALNUT & LEMON ♦ MERINGUE CAKE ♦

This rather elaborate cake makes an excellent, light addition to a tea table. Use bought lemon curd or home-made (see page 133). This cake is best eaten the same day it is made.

♦ **Preparation** 25 minutes ♦ **Cooking** 35–40 minutes ♦ **Makes** 18 cm (7 in) round cake ♦

METHOD

Heat the oven to 375°F (190°C/Gas 5). Grease and line 2 × 18 cm (7 in) round sandwich tins and brush the sides of the tins with a little oil.

Beat the egg whites until stiff. Add half the sugar and beat again until very stiff. Add the rest of the sugar and keep beating until the meringue is so stiff that it does not flow.

Chop 100 g (4 oz) of the walnuts roughly and stir into the meringue with a metal spoon. Divide the mixture between the prepared tins and smooth the tops with a palette knife.

INGREDIENTS

For the cake
10 ml (2 tsp) margarine, to grease tins
10 ml (2 tsp) oil, to oil tins
4 medium egg whites
250 g (9 oz) caster sugar
150 g (5 oz) walnuts

For the filling and topping
275 ml (½ pt) double cream
75 ml (5 tbsp) lemon curd

Continued overleaf

Bake for 35–40 minutes until firm and golden. Remove from the oven and turn out carefully on to a wire rack to cool. Peel off the lining paper carefully.

Whip the cream and fold half into the lemon curd. Use this to sandwich the meringue cakes together. Spread the rest of the cream over the top of the cake, swirling it with a round-bladed knife to make a pattern. Decorate with the remaining walnuts.

◆ WHISKY RAISIN CAKE ◆

This cake is too good to eat as an everyday family cake. It is ideal for guests who want something a little special with their tea, but not too rich and sweet.

◆ **Preparation** 12 hours or overnight to soak fruit, plus 20 minutes ◆ **Cooking** 1 hour ◆
◆ **Makes** 23 cm (9 in) round cake ◆

INGREDIENTS

225 g (8 oz) raisins
Grated rind of ½ lemon
100 ml (4 fl oz) whisky
175 g (6 oz) plain flour, sifted
15 ml (1 tbsp) baking powder
175 g (6 oz) butter, softened,
    plus 5 ml (1 tsp) to grease
    tin
175 g (6 oz) caster sugar
4 medium eggs, separated
75 g (3 oz) mixed candied peel

Pictured opposite page 112

METHOD

Soak the raisins and lemon rind in the whisky for at least 12 hours, or, if possible, overnight.

Heat the oven to 350°F (180°C/Gas 4) and grease and line a 23 cm (9 in) round tin.

Mix together the flour and baking powder. In a separate bowl, cream the butter and sugar together until light and fluffy. Beat in the egg yolks, one at a time, mixing in 15 ml (1 tbsp) of the flour with each yolk, and beating hard after each addition.

With a metal spoon, stir in the soaked lemon rind, raisins and whisky, and another 15 ml (1 tbsp) of the flour. Stir in the candied peel, and then stir in the rest of the flour.

Beat the egg whites until stiff and, with a metal spoon, fold gently into the cake mixture.

Pour into the prepared tin and bake for 1 hour until a skewer comes out clean. Remove from the oven and leave to cool in the tin for 10 minutes before turning out on to a wire rack to cool completely.

HIGH TEA SAVOURIES

High tea is traditionally quite different from afternoon tea. Afternoon tea began in the eighteenth century as an elegant social occasion for the upper and upper-middle classes, and was in fact called 'low tea' in those days. High tea probably developed with the Industrial Revolution in the nineteenth century. When the family returned hungry from work in the late afternoon, a hearty meal was prepared and eaten at about 6 o'clock. This meal would include savoury dishes such as Welsh rarebit, cold meats and pies, fish rissoles and salads, as well as home-made bread and butter, crumpets, muffins, tea breads and cakes. The meal took the place of dinner but a further light snack was eaten later in the evening.

♦ ANGELS ON HORSEBACK ♦

This is a delicious, traditional English savoury dish. Make either 4 large or 12 small Angels on horseback, as preferred. Garnish with sprigs of parsley.

♦ **Preparation and cooking** 15–20 minutes ♦ **Makes** 4 portions ♦

METHOD

Sprinkle each oyster with a few drops of lemon juice, a little cayenne and black pepper. Wind a rasher of bacon around each oyster and secure with a cocktail stick.

If you are making small Angels on horseback, quarter each slice of bread to make 12 squares, and trim off the crusts. Fry the bread in the butter or oil on both sides, or, if preferred, toast.

Place the wrapped oysters under a very hot grill and cook just long enough to crisp the bacon, turning as necessary so that all sides are cooked. Too much cooking will make the oysters hard and tough.

Lay the bacon-wrapped oysters on the fried bread or toast, 3 on each whole slice or 1 on each quarter. Serve immediately.

INGREDIENTS
12 oysters
Juice of 2–3 lemons
Cayenne pepper
Freshly ground black pepper
12 thin bacon rashers, with rinds removed
4 slices of wholewheat bread
45–60 ml (3–4 tbsp) butter or sunflower oil, to fry bread (optional)

INGREDIENTS
4 medium eggs
60 ml (4 tbsp) double cream
¾ tsp anchovy essence
24 capers, 12 chopped and 12
    left whole
Salt and freshly ground black
    pepper
Good shake of cayenne
    pepper
25 g (1 oz) butter, plus
    25–50 g (1–2 oz) to spread
    on toast
4 slices of bread
4 anchovy fillets, cut into thin
    strips

INGREDIENTS
75 g (3 oz) butter
225 g (8 oz) bacon rashers,
    with rinds removed
575–825 ml (1–1½ pt) water
5 ml (1 tsp) salt
450 g (1 lb) leeks, cut into
    2.5 cm (1 in) pieces
50 g (2 oz) plain flour
575 ml (1 pt) milk
100 g (4 oz) mature Cheddar
    cheese, grated
Pinch of ground nutmeg
Salt and freshly ground black
    pepper

◆ BOMBAY TOAST ◆

*This is an old colonial recipe which gives an unusual piquancy to
scrambled eggs.*

◆ **Preparation and cooking** 15–20 minutes ◆ **Makes** 4 portions ◆

METHOD
Beat the eggs well in a bowl. Add the cream, anchovy essence and
chopped capers, and mix well. Season with salt, pepper and cayenne.

Melt the butter in a non-stick saucepan and add the egg mixture.
Cook gently over a low heat, stirring frequently.

While the egg is cooking, toast the bread and spread generously with
butter. Place on serving plates.

Pile the cooked egg on the toast and lay the strips of anchovy fillet
across the top of each to form a lattice pattern. Place the whole capers in
between the fillets and serve immediately.

◆ CHEESY LEEKS & BACON ◆

*Serve this satisfying savoury dish on toast or with hot wholewheat rolls.
Garnish with chopped parsley.*

◆ **Preparation and cooking** 20 minutes ◆ **Makes** 4 portions ◆

METHOD
Heat the oven to 300°F (150°C/Gas 2) and put in a serving dish to warm.

Melt 25 g (1 oz) of the butter in a frying pan and fry the bacon until
just turning brown. Remove from the pan, drain on a paper towel and
cut into small pieces.

Bring the water to the boil in a medium saucepan. Add the 5 ml
(1 tsp) salt. When the water is boiling, put in the leeks and boil for 5–8
minutes, longer if you like them soft. Drain and plunge the leeks into
cold water to stop them cooking further. Drain and pat dry.

In a medium saucepan, melt the remaining butter. When it is sizzling,
add the flour, stir well to mix and cook over a moderate heat for 2–3
minutes. Remove from the heat and very gradually add the milk,
mixing carefully so that no lumps appear. When all the milk has been
added, return to the heat and bring slowly to the boil, stirring
continuously. Boil for 1–2 minutes. Lower the heat and add the cheese.
Stir to blend thoroughly and cook for a further 1–2 minutes. Add the
pinch of nutmeg and season to taste.

Add the bacon and leeks to the saucepan. Stir well to make sure that
they are evenly distributed throughout the sauce and heat until
bubbling gently. Turn into the warmed serving dish and serve at once.

◆ DEVILLED SARDINES ◆

These little marinated sardines are served on slices of toast. They make a tasty starter for a supper party as well as being an ideal dish for high tea. Decorate with sprigs of parsley or tomato slices.

◆ **Preparation and cooking** 1 hour to soak sardines, plus 15 minutes ◆
◆ **Makes** 4 portions ◆

METHOD

Carefully scrape the skin off the sardines. Split each fish down the back and remove the bones. Join the 2 halves of each fish together again and lay in a shallow dish.

Mix together the chopped shallots, lemon juice, cayenne, salt and pepper. Sprinkle over the sardines and leave to marinate for 1 hour, turning once.

Drain the sardines, pat dry with a paper towel and roll each fish lightly in the flour. Heat the oil or butter in a frying pan and fry the fish gently until browned.

Meanwhile, toast the bread and spread generously with butter. Divide the sardines into 4 and place one portion on each slice of toast. Serve immediately.

INGREDIENTS

2 × 124 g (4.37 oz) cans of sardines in oil, drained
2 shallots, chopped finely
20 ml (4 tsp) freshly squeezed lemon juice
Shake of cayenne pepper
Salt and freshly ground black pepper
30–45 ml (2–3 tbsp) plain flour
30 ml (2 tbsp) oil or butter, to fry fish
4 slices of bread
30 g (1½ oz) butter

◆ EGGS IN TUNA SAUCE ◆

This is excellent served on toast or with warm fresh bread. Hard-boiled eggs and mushrooms are combined in a delicious tuna fish sauce. Garnish with tomato slices and chopped parsley.

◆ **Preparation and cooking** 20–25 minutes ◆ **Makes** 4 portions ◆

METHOD

Melt 25 g (1 oz) of the butter in a small saucepan and cook the sliced mushrooms gently for 5–10 minutes, until soft. Remove from the pan with a slotted spoon and keep in a dish until needed.

Blend the soup with the milk in a bowl. Melt the rest of the butter in a clean saucepan and stir in the flour. Mix thoroughly and stir over a moderate heat for 2–3 minutes.

Remove from the heat and gradually add the soup and milk mixture, a very little at a time. Stir carefully to blend so that no lumps develop. When well blended, return to the heat and bring to the boil. Boil for 2–3 minutes, stirring continuously.

Warm a serving dish or individual plates. Add the mushrooms, eggs and tuna to the sauce and allow to heat through. Turn into the warmed dish or plates and serve immediately.

INGREDIENTS

50 g (2 oz) butter
50 g (2 oz) button mushrooms, sliced
200 g (7 oz) can of mushroom soup
100 ml (4 fl oz) milk
25 g (1 oz) plain flour
4 medium hard-boiled eggs, quartered
198 g (7 oz) can of tuna in oil, drained and flaked

Pictured opposite page 96

♦ EGGS POACHED WITH HAM ♦

Serve with hot buttered toast or rolls.

♦ **Preparation and cooking** 20 minutes ♦ **Makes** 4 portions ♦

INGREDIENTS
25 g (1 oz) butter
100 g (4 oz) cooked lean ham, chopped finely
10 ml (2 tsp) finely chopped parsley
4 medium eggs
Salt and freshly ground black pepper
Cayenne pepper

METHOD
Heat the oven to 350°F (180°C/Gas 4) and grease 4 ramekins or individual dishes with half the butter.

Mix the ham with the parsley. Spoon a layer of the mixture into the base of each ramekin or dish. Carefully break an egg into each, keeping the yolks whole. Sprinkle with a little salt, pepper and cayenne and place a large dot of butter on top of each.

Place the ramekins or dishes in a baking tin and surround them to half their depth with boiling water. Carefully place the baking tin in the oven and cook for about 10–15 minutes until the whites of the eggs are set.

Remove from the oven and serve immediately.

♦ KEDGEREE ♦

This is traditionally an English breakfast dish, but it also makes an excellent dish for high tea. Garnish with sprigs of parsley.

♦ **Preparation and cooking** 15 minutes ♦ **Makes** 4 portions ♦

INGREDIENTS
2 medium hard-boiled eggs
50 g (2 oz) butter
100 g (4 oz) rice, boiled and dried
450 g (1 lb) cold smoked haddock, flaked
Shake of cayenne pepper
Salt and freshly ground black pepper

METHOD
Heat the oven to 300°F (150°C/Gas 2). Put in a serving dish to warm.

Slice the egg whites and press the yolks through a sieve.

Melt the butter in a medium saucepan or frying pan. Add to it the rice, fish, egg whites, cayenne and seasoning, and stir until hot.

Turn into the serving dish. Sprinkle over the egg yolks and serve.

♦ KIDNEY PÂTE ON TOAST ♦

Garnish with parsley or cucumber slices.

♦ **Preparation and cooking** 20–25 minutes ♦ **Makes** 4 portions ♦

INGREDIENTS
6 lambs' kidneys
275 ml (½ pt) water
30 g (1½ oz) butter, plus 25–50 g (1–2 oz) to spread on toast
45 ml (3 tbsp) double cream
¾ tsp fresh lemon juice
½ tsp cayenne pepper
Salt and black pepper
4 slices of wholewheat bread

METHOD
Place the kidneys in a saucepan with the water. Bring to the boil and simmer for about 15 minutes, until tender. Drain and remove any skin and gristle from the kidneys. Mix in a blender or food processor with the butter, cream, lemon juice, cayenne, salt and black pepper.

Toast the bread and spread generously with butter. Spread the kidney pâté on the toast, and serve immediately.

KIPPER FILLETS
♦ IN CREAM ♦

This makes an ideal high tea savoury dish served with hot buttered toast or buttered wholewheat bread. It can also be served as a starter for dinners or supper parties. Use lemon twists or chopped parsley to garnish.

♦ **Preparation and cooking** 10–15 minutes ♦ **Makes** 4 portions ♦

METHOD

Melt the butter in a frying pan and fry the chopped shallots over a gentle heat until transparent, about 8–10 minutes. Add the cream and bring to the boil. Add the kipper fillets and simmer for 4–5 minutes.

Season with the nutmeg and pepper, and pour carefully into serving dishes. Serve immediately.

INGREDIENTS

30 g (1½ oz) butter
3 shallots, chopped finely
200 ml (7 fl oz) double cream
350 g (12 oz) kipper fillets, whole or broken into small pieces
Pinch of ground nutmeg
Freshly ground black pepper

MUSHROOMS & ANCHOVY
♦ CREAM ♦

This is a Cambridge College recipe from 1881. The strong salty flavour of the anchovies is softened by the cream, and for anyone who likes mushrooms this is a really tasty treat. As an alternative to fried bread, the mushrooms can be served on buttered toast. Decorate with sprigs of parsley or cucumber twists.

♦**Preparation and cooking** 25 minutes ♦ **Makes** 4 portions ♦

METHOD

Heat the oven to 325°F (170°C/Gas 3) and put in an ovenproof plate to warm.

Cut out circles from each slice of bread, using a 6–8 cm (2½–3 in) pastry cutter. Heat the butter or oil in a frying pan, and when really hot place the circles of bread in the pan and fry until golden on both sides. Drain on a paper towel and keep hot in the oven on the plate.

Heat a little more butter or oil in the pan if necessary, and put in the mushrooms. Cover and cook gently until tender, about 8–10 minutes. Season with a little salt and pepper.

Chop the anchovies if using and rub through a sieve to make a paste. Whip the cream until stiff. Thoroughly blend the anchovy paste or Gentleman's Relish with the cream.

Arrange the fried bread on serving plates and place 1 mushroom on each piece of bread. In the middle of each mushroom, place a spoonful of the anchovy cream. Serve immediately.

INGREDIENTS

12 slices of granary or wholewheat bread, each about 7 mm (¼ in) thick
60–90 ml (4–6 tbsp) butter or sunflower oil, to fry bread and mushrooms
12 large flat field mushrooms, about 6–8 cm (2½–3 in) in diameter, with their stalks removed
Salt and freshly ground black pepper
5–6 anchovies or 5 ml (1 tsp) Gentleman's Relish
45 ml (3 tbsp) double cream

INGREDIENTS

225 g (8 oz) fresh peeled
  shrimps
¼ tsp ground mace
¼ tsp ground cloves
Pinch of ground nutmeg
Salt and freshly ground black
  pepper
175 g (6 oz) butter

♦ POTTED SHRIMPS ♦

*This recipe dates back to 1830. These potted shrimps are delicious
served with wholewheat toast or rolls. Garnish with cucumber twists or
sprigs of parsley.*

♦ **Preparation and cooking** 30 minutes, plus 1–1¼ hours to chill ♦ **Makes** 4 portions ♦

METHOD

Heat the oven to 300°F (150°C/Gas 2).

Place the shrimps in a shallow baking dish and sprinkle over the
spices, salt and pepper. Melt 50 g (2 oz) of the butter in a small saucepan
and pour over the shrimps. Bake for 10–15 minutes.

Remove from the oven. Stir well and divide the shrimps between 4
ramekins or individual dishes. Chill for 30 minutes in the refrigerator.

Make clarified butter with the remaining 100 g (4 oz) butter (see
below for method). Pour over the shrimps and leave for ½–¾ hour to set
in the refrigerator.

CLARIFIED BUTTER

Place the required amount of butter in a saucepan. Heat slowly and
remove the scum as it rises. When the butter is quite clear, pour
immediately over the shrimps or whatever is being potted.

INGREDIENTS

12–15 anchovies or 15 ml
  (1 tbsp) Gentleman's Relish
30 g (1½ oz) butter, plus 65 g
  (2½ oz) to spread on toast
60 ml (4 tbsp) double cream
4 medium egg yolks,
  chopped
5 ml (1 tsp) chopped fresh
  parsley
Good pinch of cayenne
  pepper
Pinch of salt
8 slices of wholewheat bread

♦ SCOTCH WOODCOCK ♦

*This is a tasty mixture of eggs, anchovies, cream and parsley served on
toast. It should be as hot as possible when served.*

♦ **Preparation and cooking** 20 minutes ♦ **Makes** 4 portions ♦

METHOD

Chop the anchovies if using and rub through a sieve to make a paste.

In a small saucepan over a low heat, gently melt the 30 g (1½ oz)
butter. Add the cream and egg yolks and stir until the mixture thickens.
Add the parsley, cayenne and salt and blend well. Leave to simmer over
a very low heat while you make the toast.

Toast the bread and spread with butter and the anchovy paste or
Gentleman's Relish.

Bring the cream and egg mixture almost to the boil and pour on to
the toast. Cut the toast into squares or fingers and serve immediately.

♦ SCRAMBLED EGGS ♦

The secret of good scrambled eggs is slow cooking, with gentle, frequent stirring and the use of cream instead of milk. Try adding freshly chopped chives to the egg mixture before it is cooked, or chopped ham, grated cheese, sliced mushrooms, skinned and chopped tomatoes or chopped smoked salmon. Serve on toast or with bread or bread rolls.

♦ **Preparation and cooking** 15 minutes ♦ **Makes** 4 portions ♦

INGREDIENTS
8 medium eggs
150 ml (¼ pt) double cream
Salt and freshly ground black pepper
30 g (1½ oz) butter

METHOD

Beat the eggs thoroughly in a bowl. Add the cream and seasoning and beat again.

Melt the butter gently in a non-stick saucepan. Add the egg mixture, reduce the heat to low and cook, stirring the mixture frequently with a wooden spoon.

When the eggs are thickening and almost ready, about 10 minutes, remove from the heat. Leave in the pan for about 30 seconds to allow the eggs to finish cooking in their own heat, and serve immediately.

SMOKED HADDOCK ♦ ON TOAST ♦

This can be presented in a serving dish or in individual portions on toast. Fresh wholewheat rolls may be served as an accompaniment instead of toast, if desired. Garnish with sprigs of parsley.

♦ **Preparation and cooking** 30–40 minutes ♦ **Makes** 4 portions ♦

INGREDIENTS
450 g (1 lb) smoked haddock
575 ml (1 pt) milk
50 g (2 oz) butter, plus 25–50 g (1–2 oz) to spread on toast
2 shallots, chopped finely
15 ml (1 tbsp) finely chopped fresh parsley
4 medium eggs
Pinch of ground nutmeg
Shake of cayenne pepper
Freshly ground black pepper
4 slices of bread

Pictured opposite page 96

METHOD

Heat the oven to 350°F (180°C/Gas 4).

Place the haddock in an ovenproof dish with the milk and bake for 10–15 minutes. Remove from the oven, lift the fish from the juice and put on a plate, but do not throw the juice away. Remove any skin and bones and separate the fish into large flakes.

Heat the butter in a medium saucepan. Fry the shallots until transparent but not browned, about 8–10 minutes. Add the fish and parsley and heat through for 4–5 minutes.

Beat the eggs in a bowl with half the cooking juice from the fish. Add the nutmeg, cayenne and black pepper. Pour over the fish mixture in the saucepan. Cook gently, stirring carefully now and again, until the sauce thickens, about 4–5 minutes.

Toast the bread and spread generously with butter. Pile the fish sauce on to the toast and serve immediately.

INGREDIENTS

15 g ($\frac{1}{2}$ oz) butter, softened, plus 25–50 g (1–2 oz) to spread on toast

30 ml (2 tbsp) single cream

10 ml (2 tsp) chopped fresh chives or 5 ml (1 tsp) dried chives

5 ml (1 tsp) whole-grain mustard

$\frac{1}{2}$ tsp creamed horseradish

$\frac{1}{2}$ tsp freshly ground black pepper

100 g (4 oz) mature Cheddar cheese, grated

4 slices of bread

♦ WELSH RAREBIT ♦

Traditionally, Welsh rarebit does not include chives, but they do make it a very tangy, tasty dish. This is delicious served with chutneys or pickles. Garnish with cucumber twists or strips of green pepper.

♦ **Preparation and cooking** 15 minutes ♦ **Makes** 4 portions ♦

METHOD

Mix together well the butter, cream, chives, mustard, horseradish and black pepper in a bowl. When well blended, stir in the cheese and mix carefully with a wooden spoon to make sure that all the ingredients are evenly distributed.

Cut the bread into halves or quarters and toast under a grill on one side only. Spread the untoasted sides with butter and then cover with the Welsh rarebit mixture.

Put under a hot grill and cook for 4–5 minutes until the cheese bubbles, forms a skin and turns golden brown. Place on a serving dish and serve immediately.

VARIATIONS

Buck rarebit: Make exactly as for Welsh rarebit, above, but poach 4 eggs while the rarebit is being grilled, and then place 1 on each portion before serving.

Gloucestershire rarebit: Make exactly as for Welsh rarebit, above, but substitute Double Gloucester for Cheddar, and use 30–45 ml (2–3 tbsp) dry cider instead of the creamed horseradish.

High tea Clockwise from top: Eccles cakes (see page 62); Eggs in tuna sauce (see page 91); Smoked haddock on toast (see page 95); Chocolate squares (see page 60).

CHILDREN'S TEAS

Children in Victorian and Edwardian times usually had tea in the nursery with their nanny. The food was chosen to suit their tastes as well as to provide a good, nourishing meal. Today, still, children often have a meal in the mid- to late-afternoon when they return from school.

Savoury dishes, biscuits and cakes may also be chosen from the other chapters in this book, but those recipes which are most suitable for children are given here. Both traditional tea time recipes and more modern items are included. Most are fun and interesting in appearance, making them ideal for special children's tea parties.

SANDWICHES

Note: *'Makes 1 sandwich' refers to a double slice of bread, regardless of the number of cut squares, fingers, etc.*

◆ ALPHABETS ◆

The letters piped on to these tiny open sandwiches can be the initials of the children. Alternatively, numbers can be used. Garnish with cucumber twists and tomato slices.

◆ **Preparation** 20–30 minutes ◆ **Makes** About 30 alphabets ◆

METHOD
Spread the bread with the butter. Place the chopped ham or pork slices on 5 of the slices of bread. Place the processed cheese slices on the other 5.

INGREDIENTS
10 thin slices of bread, of various kinds, if liked
60–75 g (2½–3 oz) butter, softened
5–6 large slices of chopped ham or pork
5 slices of processed cheese
50 g (2 oz) cream cheese
15 ml (1 tbsp) milk

Continued overleaf

Afternoon tea Clockwise from top: Old English cider cake with cream cheese and ginger topping (see page 77); Éclairs (see page 63); Madeira cake (see page 75).

Trim off all the crusts and cut the slices into several pieces, using different-shaped pastry cutters. Try to waste as little as possible.

Beat the cream cheese and milk together. Put in a piping bag with a small nozzle, or make a small cone from greaseproof paper. Put the cheese mixture inside, and snip a tiny piece off the end if using a paper cone.

Carefully pipe a letter on to each shape. Arrange the shapes on a serving plate.

BANANA & CHOCOLATE
♦ SANDWICHES ♦

Children love the combination of banana and chocolate, and this sandwich is quick and easy to make.

♦ **Preparation** 7–8 minutes ♦ **Makes** 2 sandwiches ♦

METHOD

Spread the bread with the butter. Slice the bananas and keep back 4 slices for decoration. Lay the rest neatly over 2 slices of bread.

Carefully scatter a thick layer of the grated chocolate over the banana. Place the other 2 slices of bread on top and press down firmly.

Trim off the crusts, cut into 4 triangles and arrange neatly on individual plates. Decorate each sandwich with one of the reserved slices of banana.

INGREDIENTS
4 slices of brown bread
25 g (1 oz) butter, softened
2 large ripe bananas
75 g (3 oz) dark or milk
   chocolate, grated

CHEESY PEANUT BUTTER
♦ SANDWICHES ♦

Sliced cucumber can be used instead of lettuce in this rich and tasty sandwich, if liked.

♦ **Preparation** 5 minutes ♦ **Makes** 2 sandwiches ♦

METHOD

Spread the bread with the butter and then the peanut butter. Place a layer of cheddar cheese over 2 of the slices.

Lay the shredded lettuce on top of the cheese and press the other 2 slices of bread down on top. Trim off the crusts and cut into 4 triangles.

INGREDIENTS
4 slices of granary or nutty
   bread
25 g (1 oz) butter, softened
60 ml (4 tbsp) peanut butter
75 g (3 oz) Cheddar cheese,
   grated
A few lettuce leaves,
   shredded

COLD SAUSAGE
♦ SANDWICHES ♦

A little grated cheese and some shredded lettuce can be added to this sandwich if liked, and mayonnaise can be used instead of tomato ketchup.

♦ **Preparation** 5 minutes ♦ **Makes** 2 sandwiches ♦

METHOD

Spread the bread with the butter. Slice the sausages lengthways to make long, thin, flat strips.

Spread 2 slices of bread with tomato ketchup or relish and lay the slices of sausage on top. Press the other 2 slices down on top. Trim off the crusts and cut into 4 squares.

INGREDIENTS
4 slices of bread
25 g (1 oz) butter, softened
2 large, cold cooked sausages
10 ml (2 tsp) tomato ketchup or relish

♦ SANDWICH KEBABS ♦

The fillings for these sandwiches threaded on to kebab sticks need to be the type that will not fall out easily, such as liver pâté, salmon and mayonnaise, processed cheese, cream cheese and meat. Many other items can be threaded on to these kebabs: try radishes, tomato slices, dates, apple pieces or slices of banana.

♦ **Preparation** 15–20 minutes ♦ **Makes** 4 kebabs ♦

METHOD

Spread the bread with the butter. On 1 slice of wholewheat bread, spread the liver pâté. Press the other slice of wholewheat on top and trim off the crusts. Cut into 4 squares.

Spread the Marmite on to 1 slice of granary bread and lay the cheese on top. Press a second slice of granary bread on top, trim off the crusts and cut into 4 triangles.

Mash the sardines with the egg and mix in the mayonnaise. Season with salt and pepper. Spread on to the third slice of granary bread and sandwich with the last slice. Trim off the crusts and cut into 4 squares.

Lay the sliced meat on to 1 slice of white bread. Press the other slice on top, trim off the crusts and cut into 4 triangles.

On to each kebab stick, thread 1 cube of pineapple, 1 liver pâté sandwich, 1 slice of cucumber or green pepper, 1 cheese and Marmite sandwich, 1 slice of carrot, 1 sardine and egg sandwich and another cube of pineapple. Lay the kebabs on a serving plate or individual plates, and cover with cling film if not serving immediately.

INGREDIENTS
8 slices of bread, 2 wholewheat, 4 granary and 2 white
50 g (2 oz) butter, softened
25 g (1 oz) liver pâté
$\frac{1}{2}$ tsp Marmite
25 g (1 oz) Cheddar cheese, sliced
2 sardines, drained and boned
1 medium hard-boiled egg, shelled and mashed
5 ml (1 tsp) mayonnaise
Salt and freshly ground black pepper
2 slices of cold meat of your choice
4 kebab sticks (wooden if liked)
8 cubes of pineapple
4 thick slices of cucumber or green pepper
4 slices of carrot

SAVOURY DISHES

INGREDIENTS
25 g (1 oz) butter, softened
1 medium egg, beaten
15 ml (1 tbsp) double cream
Salt and freshly ground black
    pepper
50 g (2 oz) ham, chopped
    finely
2 slices of wholewheat bread

◆ EGG & HAM TOASTS ◆

Children love scrambled egg and it is soft and easy to eat. The addition of ham makes this a more interesting dish. Garnish each toast with a slice of radish.

◆ **Preparation and cooking** 15–20 minutes ◆ **Makes** 8 small toasts ◆

METHOD

Melt 15 g (½ oz) of the butter in a saucepan. Beat together the egg, cream, salt and pepper and add to the pan. Scramble the egg slowly, stirring frequently. Stir in the chopped ham.

When the eggs are thickening and almost ready, remove the pan from the heat and allow the eggs to finish cooking in their own heat.

Meanwhile, lightly toast the bread. Spread with the remaining butter and trim off the crusts. Spread the egg over the toast, and cut each slice into 4 squares.

INGREDIENTS
4 medium eggs
30 ml (2 tbsp) milk
Salt and freshly ground black
    pepper
50 g (2 oz) butter, softened
8 large slices of granary bread
12 thin slices of luncheon
    meat or salami sausage
24 cocktail sticks

◆ EGG & MEAT BOATS ◆

The boats are made from toast covered with scrambled egg and the sails are made from thinly sliced luncheon meat or salami sausage. Garnish the dish with sprigs of parsley.

◆ **Preparation and cooking** 20–25 minutes ◆ **Makes** 24 boats ◆

METHOD

Beat together the eggs, milk and seasoning. Melt a little of the butter in a non-stick saucepan and add the egg mixture. Cook gently, stirring frequently, until scrambled. Remove from the heat and leave to cool.

Lightly toast the bread, trim off the crusts and spread with the remaining butter. Spread the cold egg over each finger and cut each slice into 3 fingers.

Cut the slices of luncheon meat or salami in half, and thread a cocktail stick through the top and bottom of each half to form sails.

Arrange the toast fingers on a serving dish or tray. Press a cocktail stick sail into the middle of each.

◆ PARTY BURGERS ◆

These are so full of goodies that they need to be eaten with a knife and fork.

◆ **Preparation and cooking** 25–30 minutes ◆ **Makes** 6 burgers ◆

METHOD

Heat the oven to 325°F (170°C/Gas 3).

Heat the oil in a frying pan and fry the onion rings over a gentle heat until soft and slightly browned, about 10–15 minutes. Remove from the pan with a slotted spoon and drain on a paper towel. Keep hot in the oven in an ovenproof dish.

Fry or grill the beefburgers and bacon on both sides, about 10–15 minutes. Remove from the pan, drain and keep hot in the oven. Heat the baked beans in a small saucepan.

Slice each bun in half across the middle. Lay a beefburger on the bottom half of each bun and then add a spoonful of baked beans, a piece of bacon, and a handful of grated cheese. Top with the onion rings. Place the other halves of the buns on top and serve immediately.

INGREDIENTS

About 30 ml (2 tbsp) oil, to fry onions and meat

3 medium onions, sliced into rings

6 beefburgers

6 rashers of bacon

200 g (7 oz) can of baked beans in tomato sauce

6 sesame buns

100 g (4 oz) Cheddar cheese, grated

SAUSAGE, BACON & CHEESE ◆ KEBABS ◆

To serve these colourful kebabs, insert them into half apples or grapefruit, placed cut side down on a pretty serving plate.

◆ **Preparation and cooking** 35–40 minutes ◆ **Makes** 24 kebabs ◆

METHOD

Grill the sausages. Cut each into 3 pieces and keep hot. Grill the rolled bacon until well cooked but not too crispy, and keep hot. Cut the cheese into small chunks.

On to each cocktail stick thread a piece of cheese, a piece of sausage, another piece of cheese, a roll of bacon, and then finally another piece of cheese.

INGREDIENTS

225 g (8 oz) chipolata sausages

24 rashers of bacon, each rolled up and secured, with a cocktail stick

225 g (8 oz) cheese, of different varieties, if liked, to add colour

24 cocktail sticks

INGREDIENTS

25 g (1 oz) butter
1 medium onion, chopped
    finely
50 g (2 oz) celery, sliced thinly
225 g (8 oz) can of peeled
    tomatoes
½ tsp mustard
4–5 drops of Worcester sauce
Salt and freshly ground black
    pepper
½ tsp caster or demerara sugar
Pinch of mixed herbs
450 g (1 lb) cooked sausages,
    cold or hot

SAUSAGES WITH
◆ TOMATO DIP ◆

*This dip goes well with most meats, so it can also be served with cooked
chicken or turkey, chunks of ham or crispy lamb cutlets. Strips of
vegetable can be added for colour.*

◆ **Preparation and cooking** 25–30 minutes ◆ **Makes** 4–6 portions ◆

METHOD

Melt the butter in a medium saucepan. Fry the onion and celery for
about 10 minutes, until soft but not brown. Add all the remaining
ingredients except the sausages and cook for a further 8–10 minutes
over a low heat.

    Turn into a serving bowl. Stand the bowl on a larger serving dish or
tray and arrange the sausages around the bowl.

BISCUITS, CAKES & JELLIES

INGREDIENTS

For the cake base
5 ml (1 tsp) margarine, to
    grease tin
4 medium eggs
100 g (4 oz) caster sugar
75 g (3 oz) plain flour, sifted
50 g (2 oz) butter, melted

For the icing and decoration
30 g (1½ oz) butter
75 g (3 oz) icing sugar
10 ml (2 tsp) water
Few drops of pink food
    colouring
32 chocolate peppermint
    creams

◆ CATS' WHISKERS ◆

*These are squares of sponge cake iced with pink glacé icing, and with
little cats' faces on top made from chocolate peppermint creams. The
icing and the cats' eyes, noses and whiskers do not have to be pink, but
can be any colour of your choice.*

◆ **Preparation** 45–50 minutes ◆ **Cooking** 25–30 minutes ◆ **Makes** 21 cakes ◆

METHOD

Heat the oven to 350°F (180°C/Gas 4) and grease and line a 28 × 18 cm
(11 × 7 in) shallow tin.

    Beat the eggs and sugar together in a bowl set over a saucepan of
simmering water. Beat until the mixture is thick and pale yellow, and
leaves a trail when the beater is lifted. This will take 6–8 minutes.

    Remove the bowl from the heat and continue beating until cold.
Using a metal spoon, gently fold in two-thirds of the flour. Then, fold
in the melted butter and the remaining flour.

    Pour into the prepared tin and bake for 25–30 minutes until firm to
the touch and light golden. Remove from the oven and turn out on to a
wire rack to cool. Remove the lining paper, and turn over so that the
underside is uppermost.

    For the icing, cream the butter, icing sugar and hot water together
until light and fluffy. Add enough pink food colouring to give a delicate

pink. Keep back 15 ml (1 tbsp) of the icing and use the rest to spread all over the cake. Trim the edges with a sharp knife and mark a pattern all over with the prongs of a fork.

Cut the cake into 3 lengths and cut each length into 7 pieces. Lay a peppermint cream in the middle of each piece. Cut the 11 remaining peppermint creams into 4 neat quarters. Place 2 quarters on each piece, just touching the peppermint cream at an angle, to form the cats' ears.

Take a piping bag with a size 12 nozzle, or make a small cone from greaseproof paper. Put the remaining icing inside. Cut a tiny piece off the bottom if using a paper cone, and carefully pipe 2 eyes, a nose and whiskers on to each peppermint cream cat's face.

◆ CHOCOLATE CRISPIES ◆

These are made from a mixture of rice crispies or cornflakes, chocolate, butter and syrup. They are easy enough for the children to make.

◆ **Preparation and cooking** 10–15 minutes, plus 30 minutes to chill ◆
◆ **Makes** 14–16 crispies ◆

INGREDIENTS
50 g (2 oz) butter or margarine, plus 5 ml (1 tsp) to grease baking tray
50 ml (2 fl oz) syrup
100 g (4 oz) plain chocolate
75 g (3 oz) rice crispies or cornflakes

METHOD
Grease a large baking tray or place 15–16 paper cases in patty tins.

In a saucepan, melt the fat, syrup and chocolate together over a low heat. Add the rice crispies or cornflakes and mix well so that they are all coated with the chocolate mixture.

Place spoonfuls of the mixture on the tray or into the paper cases and form each into a neat cluster. Leave for about 30 minutes to set in the refrigerator and then remove carefully from the tray or patty tins.

◆ CHOCOLATE FUDGE CAKE ◆

If you feel that this cake is too rich to be cut into large fingers, cut into smaller pieces or cubes.

◆ **Preparation and cooking** 10–15 minutes, plus 1 hour to chill ◆ **Makes** 14 fingers ◆

INGREDIENTS
50 g (2 oz) butter or margarine, plus 5 ml (1 tsp) to grease tin
45 ml (3 tbsp) syrup
200 g (7 oz) plain chocolate
225 g (8 oz) digestive or ginger biscuits, crushed very finely
50 g (2 oz) raisins

METHOD
Grease and line an 18 cm (7 in) square tin.

In a saucepan, melt the fat, syrup and chocolate together over a low heat. Add the biscuit crumbs and raisins and mix thoroughly to blend all the ingredients together.

Turn into the prepared tin and smooth the top with a palette knife. Leave for about 1 hour to set in the refrigerator and then cut into 14 fingers.

INGREDIENTS

5 ml (1 tsp) margarine, to
  grease baking tray
75 g (3 oz) plain chocolate
30 ml (2 tbsp) evaporated
  milk
150 g (5 oz) desiccated
  coconut
15–30 ml (1–2 tbsp) icing
  sugar

♦ CHOCOLATE MUNCHIES ♦

Easy and quick to make, these can be eaten as little cakes or sweets.

♦ **Preparation and cooking** 10–15 minutes, plus ¾–1 hour to chill ♦
♦ **Makes** 12 munchies ♦

METHOD

Grease a baking tray.

Break the chocolate into small pieces and put in a bowl with the milk. Set the bowl over a saucepan of gently simmering water and stir occasionally until melted.

Remove the bowl from the heat and stir in the coconut. Divide into 12 equal portions. Shape into balls. Toss each ball in icing sugar and place on the prepared tray. Leave in the refrigerator for ¾–1 hour to set.

INGREDIENTS

150 ml (¼ pt) double cream
575 ml (1 pt) vanilla or
  raspberry ice cream
450 g (1 lb) fresh fruit of
  choice, peeled, cored and
  pipped as necessary
Candied or fresh fruit, or
  pistachio nuts, to decorate
  sundaes

♦ FRUIT SUNDAES ♦

Raspberries, strawberries and peaches are delicious with ice cream, but loganberries, bananas, blackcurrants, mango and pineapple are all very good too.

♦ **Preparation** 10–15 minutes ♦ **Makes** 4 sundaes ♦

METHOD

Whip the cream until stiff and put in a piping bag.

Place a scoop of ice cream in 4 individual sundae glasses. Next, spoon in a layer of fruit, crushed if using strawberries, raspberries or loganberries; sliced if using peaches, bananas, mango or pineapple.

Spoon another scoop of ice cream on top. Then, pipe cream over the top and decorate each sundae with a piece of fruit and/or nuts.

INGREDIENTS

5 ml (1 tsp) margarine, to
  grease tin
40 ml (2½ tbsp) golden syrup
150 ml (¼ pt) milk
225 g (8 oz) self-raising flour,
  sifted
Pinch of salt
5 ml (1 tsp) bicarbonate of
  soda
50 g (2 oz) sultanas

♦ GOLDEN TEA BREAD ♦

This tea bread is light and soft and should be spread with butter and jam.

♦ **Preparation** 10 minutes ♦ **Cooking** 1 hour ♦
♦ **Makes** 18 cm (7 in) round cake or 900 g (2 lb) loaf ♦

METHOD

Heat the oven to 350°F (180°C/Gas 4) and grease and line an 18 cm (7 in) round tin or a 900 g (2 lb) loaf tin.

In a medium saucepan, warm the syrup and milk together over a low heat. Add all the other ingredients and mix well.

Pour into the prepared tin and bake for 1 hour until a skewer comes out clean. Remove from the oven and turn on to a wire rack to cool.

◆ JELLY WHIP ◆

*Children of all ages love this. If you prefer the whip to be a little softer,
add a little more evaporated milk.*

◆ **Preparation** 40–45 minutes, plus 1 hour to set ◆ **Makes** 6–8 portions ◆

METHOD

Dissolve the jelly in the water and mix well. Leave until just
beginning to set, about 30–40 minutes, and then beat in the evaporated
milk, with an electric beater if you have one. The mixture expands in
volume so use a fairly large container. Beat well until it is thick and
fairly stiff.

Pour into a 575 ml (1 pt) mould or bowl and leave in the refrigerator
to set for about 1 hour. To turn out, if using a mould, dip the mould
quickly in hot water to about half-way up the sides. Give a good shake,
place a bowl or serving dish over the top and invert both. The jelly
should slide out easily.

INGREDIENTS

1 cube of jelly (any flavour)
275 ml (½ pt) hot water
200 g (7 oz) can of evaporated
  milk

◆ SHORTCAKE BISCUITS ◆

*These biscuits are soft and crumbly and are a great favourite with
young children.*

◆ **Preparation** 15 minutes ◆ **Cooking** 30–35 minutes ◆ **Makes** 8 biscuits ◆

METHOD

Heat the oven to 375°F (190°C/Gas 5) and grease 2 baking trays.

Cream the butter and sugar together until light and fluffy. Mix in the
vanilla. With a wooden spoon, mix in the flour and cornflour to form a
fairly stiff paste.

Put the mixture in a piping bag with a star nozzle, and pipe 8 circles
on to the prepared trays. Start from the middle and work out to the
edge of the circle in a spiral.

Bake for 30–35 minutes until pale golden. Remove from the oven
and leave to cool on the trays for 2–3 minutes before transferring
carefully to a wire rack to cool. Dredge with the icing sugar.

INGREDIENTS

100 g (4 oz) butter, softened,
  plus 10 ml (2 tsp) to grease
  baking trays
25 g (1 oz) caster sugar
½ tsp vanilla essence
85 g (3½ oz) plain flour, sifted
15 g (½ oz) cornflour
15 ml (1 tbsp) icing sugar

WEDDING &
CELEBRATION TEAS

Food for a wedding reception tea or other celebration needs to be very special, impressive in appearance, delicate in flavour and easy to eat with the fingers. Decorate the table with beautiful flowers, choosing ones that tone in with the bride's colour scheme if for a wedding. Everything should look fresh, pure and very elegant. Arrange the food carefully, garnishing it with watercress, mustard and cress, lemon twists and fruit so that it looks fresh and appetizing. Any pastries and petits fours should remain covered with foil until the last possible minute.

CANAPÉS

INGREDIENTS
4 slices of wholewheat bread, toasted and with the crusts removed
75 g (3 oz) cream cheese
1 small shallot, minced or chopped finely
1 medium egg, beaten
Few drops of tabasco sauce

♦ CREAM CHEESE CANAPÉS ♦

These need to be prepared at the very last minute and served immediately. Garnish with sprigs of parsley.

♦ **Preparation and cooking** 15–20 minutes ♦ **Makes** 16 canapés ♦

METHOD

Heat the oven to 375°F (190°C/Gas 5). Cut each slice of toast into 4.

Mix together the cream cheese, chopped shallot, egg and tabasco sauce in a bowl. Beat until light and fluffy. Spread on to the squares of toast and place on a baking tray. Warm a serving dish ready.

Bake the canapés for 5–10 minutes until they are just beginning to turn brown. Remove from the oven, transfer to the warmed serving dish and serve at once.

SALAMI & CUCUMBER
◆ CANAPÉS ◆

This topping may be served on round savoury biscuits or circles of toast instead of bread, if liked.

◆ **Preparation** 10 minutes ◆ **Makes** 16 canapés ◆

METHOD

Using a pastry cutter the same size as the slices of salami, cut out circles from the bread. Spread each carefully with the butter and a little mustard.

Lay 1 slice of salami on each circle of bread. Cut the slices of cucumber in half and lay 3 halves over the top of each canapé, slightly overlapping to produce a fan-like effect.

INGREDIENTS

7 slices of firm granary bread
50 g (2 oz) butter, softened
5–10 ml (1–2 tsp) whole-grain mustard
16 slices of salami sausage
½ cucumber, peeled and sliced neatly

◆ SARDINE CANAPÉS ◆

This is one of the prettiest canapés to serve at a tea party.

◆ **Preparation** 10–15 minutes ◆ **Makes** 16 canapés ◆

METHOD

Spread the bread with the butter. Cut each slice into 4 triangles.

Drain and remove the bones from the sardines and mash the flesh in a bowl with the black pepper, lemon juice and parsley.

Spread the mixture on to the triangles of bread. Place 1 slice of egg on top of each, and then lay on a rolled-up anchovy.

INGREDIENTS

4 slices of white bread, with the crusts removed
50 g (2 oz) unsalted butter
124 g (4.37 oz) can of sardines
Freshly ground black pepper
¼ tsp fresh lemon juice
10 ml (2 tsp) chopped fresh parsley
3 medium hard-boiled eggs, sliced thinly
16 anchovy fillets, rolled-up

◆ SHRIMP CANAPÉS ◆

This topping is deliciously spicy, and can also be served on savoury biscuits or toast if liked. Garnish with chopped parsley.

◆ **Preparation and cooking** 10 minutes ◆ **Makes** 16 canapés ◆

METHOD

Fry the slices of bread in the oil or butter on both sides. Drain and cut each slice of fried bread into 4 squares.

Melt the butter in a small saucepan over a low heat. When the foam subsides, add the shrimps, curry powder, cayenne, salt, lemon juice and cream, and simmer gently for 3–4 minutes.

Remove the shrimps from the pan with a slotted spoon and lay on the squares of fried bread. Place on a serving dish and serve at once.

INGREDIENTS

4 slices of white bread, with the crusts removed
30 ml (2 tbsp) oil or butter, to fry bread
50 g (2 oz) butter
100 g (4 oz) fresh or frozen peeled shrimps
¼ tsp curry powder
Pinch of cayenne pepper
Pinch of salt
10 ml (2 tsp) freshly squeezed lemon juice
15 ml (1 tbsp) double cream

OTHER IDEAS FOR
♦ CANAPÉS ♦

The base of these canapés can be small savoury biscuits, bread, fried bread or toast cut into different fancy shapes. The toppings should be carefully chosen for their colour and texture. Use different shapes and colours for an appetizing and attractive effect.

1 Round savoury biscuits topped with slices of firm tomato. Pipe a little cream cheese through a star nozzle on to the middle of each.
2 Triangles or diamonds of wholewheat bread topped with smoked salmon. Place tiny triangles of lemon and a parsley sprig on top.
3 Savoury biscuits topped with neat squares of liver pâté. Lay a slice of stuffed olive or a few capers on top of each.
4 Mildly flavoured savoury biscuits spread with cream cheese and topped with a spoonful of caviare or lump fish roe (Danish caviare).
5 Squares of fried bread with a topping of tuna fish, drained and mixed with a little sour cream or mayonnaise, and garnished with mint.
6 Squares or triangles of wholewheat toast spread with butter and a little mustard, and topped with neat squares or triangles of ham. Lay an asparagus tip in the middle of each.

SANDWICHES

Note: *'Makes 1 sandwich' refers to a double slice of bread, regardless of the number of cut squares, fingers, etc.*

♦ CAVIARE SANDWICHES ♦

Lump fish roe (Danish caviare) can be used as a substitute for caviare if desired. Decorate with lemon twists.

♦ **Preparation** 10 minutes ♦ **Makes** 5 sandwiches ♦

INGREDIENTS
50 g (2 oz) butter
65 ml (2½ fl oz) double cream
¼ tsp mustard
Very small pinch of cayenne pepper
Salt and freshly ground black pepper
10 slices of white or brown bread
75 g (3 oz) caviare
Juice of ½ lemon

METHOD
Cream the butter until soft and fluffy. Whip the cream until stiff and add to the butter. Mix well with a wooden spoon. Add the mustard and cayenne, and add salt and pepper to taste.

Spread the bread with the butter and cream mixture. Spread half the slices lightly with the caviare and sprinkle with a little lemon juice. Press the other slices of bread down on top.

Trim off the crusts and cut into neat squares or triangles.

HAM & AVOCADO
◆ SANDWICHES ◆

This is a delicious combination of flavours. The avocado must be ripe and soft, but not mushy. Garnish with cucumber twists.

◆ **Preparation** 10 minutes ◆ **Makes** 5 sandwiches ◆

METHOD

Mash the avocado and mix with the chopped shallot, salt and pepper. Spread on half the slices of bread. Lay slices of ham on top of the avocado mixture and then the shredded lettuce. Sprinkle with salt.

Spread the other slices of bread with the mustard butter and lay on top of the lettuce. Trim off the crusts and cut into triangles.

INGREDIENTS

1 ripe avocado, peeled and stoned
1 shallot, chopped finely
Salt and freshly ground black pepper
10 slices of brown bread
350 g (12 oz) sliced ham
A few lettuce leaves, shredded
65–75 g (2½–3 oz) mustard butter, softened (see page 36)

◆ OYSTER SANDWICHES ◆

Slices of this chilled oyster mould can also be served as toppings for canapés, if liked. Garnish with parsley or cucumber twists.

◆ **Preparation and cooking** 5 minutes, plus ¾–1 hour to chill ◆ **Makes** 5 sandwiches ◆

METHOD

Grease a 150 ml (¼ pt) bowl or mould. Put the oysters, 25 g (1 oz) of the butter, the breadcrumbs, cream, egg and seasoning together in a small saucepan. Bring to the boil and stir for 3–4 minutes. Turn the mixture into the bowl or mould and chill for ¾–1 hour.

Spread the bread with the remaining butter. Turn out the chilled oyster mixture and slice thinly. Lay slices on half the bread and press the other slices of bread on top. Trim off the crusts and cut into fingers.

INGREDIENTS

5 ml (1 tsp) margarine, to grease bowl or mould
40 oysters
150 g (5 oz) butter, softened
20 ml (4 tsp) very fine breadcrumbs
60 ml (4 tbsp) double cream
2 medium eggs, beaten
Salt and freshly ground black pepper
10 slices of brown bread

◆ SHRIMP SANDWICHES ◆

Fresh shrimps obviously have the best flavour, but frozen ones can be used instead. Decorate with lemon twists or cucumber slices.

◆ **Preparation** 10 minutes ◆ **Makes** 5 sandwiches ◆

METHOD

Pat the shrimps dry with a paper towel to remove any water.

Whip the cream until stiff and mix in the lemon juice and seasoning. Mix the shrimps in gently, making sure that they are distributed evenly throughout the cream.

Spread the bread with the butter and spread the shrimp cream on to half the slices of bread. Press the other slices on top and cut into triangles.

INGREDIENTS

100 g (4 oz) fresh, or frozen and thawed, peeled shrimps
100 ml (4 fl oz) double cream
½ tsp freshly squeezed lemon juice
Salt and freshly ground black pepper
10 thin slices of brown bread
65 g (2½ oz) butter, softened

SAVOURY DISHES

INGREDIENTS

For the pastry cases
½ quantity puff pastry, using 225 g (8 oz) flour (see page 137)
10 ml (2 tsp) margarine, to grease baking trays
50–75 g (2–3 oz) flour, to flour board
1 medium egg, beaten, to glaze pastry

For the filling
25 g (1 oz) butter
25 g (1 oz) plain flour
290 g (10.2 oz) can of mushroom or chicken soup
Salt and freshly ground black pepper
Pinch of cayenne pepper
225 g (8 oz) cooked chicken, cut into small pieces
225 g (8 oz) sweetcorn

Pictured opposite page 113

◆ CHICKEN VOL-AU-VENTS ◆

These puff pastry cases do not have to contain chicken filling: try shrimps in white sauce; ham and mushrooms in a cheesy sauce; or tuna chopped egg and green peppers in white sauce. Decorate with sprigs of parsley, strips of red pepper or tomato slices.

◆ **Preparation** 30 minutes, plus 4 hours for pastry ◆ **Cooking** 15–20 minutes ◆
◆ **Makes** 20 vol-au-vents ◆

METHOD

Make the pastry as on page 137 and chill for 30 minutes.

Heat the oven to 450°F (230°C/Gas 8) and grease 2 baking trays.

Roll out the pastry on a floured board to a thickness of 2 cm (¾ in). Using a 2.5–4 cm (1–1½ in) pastry cutter dipped in flour, carefully press circles out of the pastry. Place the pastry shapes on the prepared trays and brush with beaten egg. Using a smaller cutter, also dipped in flour, press into the middle of the pastry shape to about half its depth.

Bake for 15–20 minutes until golden. Remove from the oven and transfer to a wire rack to cool. When cool, carefully remove the lids from the cases and scoop out the soft pastry inside.

Make the filling while the pastry cases are cooling. Melt the butter in a medium saucepan. Add the flour and mix quickly into the butter. Cook for 2–3 minutes over a moderate heat. Remove from the heat and very gradually add the soup, stirring until the sauce is smooth. Return to the heat and bring to the boil, stirring all the time, until the sauce thickens. Season to taste with salt, pepper and cayenne, and leave the sauce to cool.

When cool, add the chopped chicken and sweetcorn to the sauce and stir carefully so that the ingredients are evenly distributed. Spoon the mixture carefully into the pastry cases and replace the lid of each.

CUCUMBER & MACKEREL
♦ RINGS ♦

These look very pretty and are light and tasty. The rings of cucumber form an ideal base for the fish pâté. Top each with a sprig of parsley or a strip of red pepper, to garnish.

♦ **Preparation** 15–20 minutes ♦ **Makes** 20 rings ♦

METHOD

Pull away the skin and any bones from the mackerel. Flake the flesh into a plate.

Cream the butter until soft and fluffy, and then beat in the cream cheese. Stir in the flaked fish, lemon juice and chives and add salt and pepper to taste. Beat thoroughly to give a smooth, well blended pâté.

Slice the cucumber into rings, 2 cm (¾ in) thick. With a teaspoon, scoop out some of the flesh in the middle of each ring, to about half the depth.

Pile spoonfuls of the pâté into the hollow of each cucumber ring and arrange on a serving plate.

INGREDIENTS

225 g (8 oz) smoked mackerel fillets (about 2)
50 g (2 oz) butter, softened
100 g (4 oz) cream cheese
Juice of ½ lemon
10 ml (2 tsp) chopped fresh chives
Salt and freshly ground black pepper
1 cucumber, washed and dried

Pictured opposite page 113

♦ HAM & LIVER PUFFS ♦

The filling of these can be varied: try a mixture of chopped chicken or turkey mixed with liver pâté, or chopped mushrooms and chopped ham mixed with cream cheese. Garnish with sprigs of parsley or watercress.

♦ **Preparation** 30 minutes, plus 4 hours for pastry ♦ **Cooking** 10–12 minutes ♦
♦ **Makes** 20 puffs ♦

METHOD

Make the pastry as on page 137 and chill for 30 minutes.

Heat the oven to 450°F (230°C/Gas 8) and grease a baking tray.

Roll out the pastry on a floured board to a rectangle measuring 25 × 20 cm (10 × 8 in). Cut into 20 squares.

Mix together the chopped ham, gherkin, liver sausage and black pepper. Place spoonfuls of the mixture on the middle of each little pastry square.

Brush the edges of the pastry with milk and fold over to form triangles. Seal the edges firmly and brush the top of each puff with milk to glaze.

Place on the prepared tray and bake for 10–12 minutes until well risen and golden brown. Remove from the oven and transfer carefully to a wire rack to cool. Serve on a plate.

INGREDIENTS

¼ quantity puff pastry, using 100 g (4 oz) flour (see page 137)
5 ml (1 tsp) margarine, to grease baking tray
50–75 g (2–3 oz) flour, to flour board
100 g (4 oz) lean ham, chopped finely
15 ml (1 tbsp) finely chopped gherkins
50 g (2 oz) liver sausage
Freshly ground black pepper
15–30 ml (1–2 tbsp) milk

INGREDIENTS

100 g (4 oz) butter, softened
30 ml (2 tbsp) double cream
50 g (2 oz) black olives,
  stoned and chopped very
  finely
Freshly ground black pepper
5 ml (1 tsp) freshly squeezed
  lemon juice
6 slices of white or brown
  bread
3–4 punnets of mustard and
  cress

◆ OLIVE BUTTER PINWHEELS ◆

*These are rolled-up slices of bread, sliced like a tiny Swiss roll, with a
lovely filling of olive butter and mustard and cress.*

◆ **Preparation** 15 minutes ◆ **Makes** 36 pinwheels ◆

METHOD

Cream the butter until light and fluffy. Mix in the cream, olives,
black pepper and lemon juice and beat until well blended and smooth.

Spread the bread with the olive butter. Scatter the cress on top. Roll
each slice up like a Swiss roll and secure with a cocktail stick. Wrap in
cling film and chill until required.

When ready to serve, unwrap the rolls and remove the cocktail sticks,
and slice each roll into 6 little pinwheels. Lay them on a serving dish, cut
sides uppermost.

INGREDIENTS

350 g (12 oz) sliced smoked
  salmon
85 g (3½ oz) unsalted butter,
  softened
15 ml (1 tbsp) freshly
  squeezed lemon juice
100 g (4 oz) cream cheese
Salt and freshly ground black
  pepper
15–30 ml (1–2 tbsp) single
  cream (optional)
6 slices of brown bread, with
  the crusts removed

SMOKED SALMON
◆ PINWHEELS ◆

*These little pinwheels are spread with smoked salmon pâté and filled
with sliced smoked salmon. Garnish with sprigs of parsley and
lemon twists.*
You will need a blender or liquidizer for this recipe.

◆ **Preparation** 25–30 minutes ◆ **Makes** 36 pinwheels ◆

METHOD

Remove any skin and bones from the salmon. To make the pâté,
place 100 g (4 oz) of the salmon in a blender or liquidizer, with 25 g
(1 oz) of the butter, the lemon juice, cream cheese, salt and pepper.
Blend until smooth. If the mixture is too stiff, blend in a little cream.

Spread the bread with the rest of the butter, and then spread on a
layer of the pâté. Over this lay the slices of smoked salmon and a
sprinkling of black pepper.

Roll the slices of bread up carefully and wrap in cling film. Pack in a
container, close together so that they hold each other in place, and chill
until needed.

When ready to serve, unwrap the rolls and slice each into 6 little
pinwheels. Lay them on a serving dish, cut sides uppermost.

Fancy & party cakes Top left: Coffee & walnut cake (see page 84); Top right: Strawberry shortcake (see page 87); Centre:
Whisky raisin cake (see page 88); Bottom: Baked cheesecake (see page 84).

BISCUITS, CAKES & GÂTEAUX

◆ AMOURETTES ◆

These lovely little tarts are boat-shaped pastry cases filled with cherries and decorated with a little cream. Other fruit such as strawberries, redcurrants or mandarin oranges can be used instead of the cherries if desired.

◆ **Preparation** ½–¾ hour, plus 1 hour to chill ◆ **Cooking** 10 minutes ◆ **Makes** 14 tarts ◆

METHOD

Place the flour in a bowl. Make a well in the middle and place the butter, sugar, egg yolks and vanilla into it. Using a fork, mix all the ingredients together until well blended, gradually drawing in the flour to make a soft dough. Knead lightly for a few minutes in the bowl until smooth. Chill for 1 hour.

Heat the oven to 375°F (190°C/Gas 5) and grease 14 boat-shaped tins.

Roll out the pastry thinly on a floured board. Use to line the prepared tins. Press a piece of greaseproof paper into each and place a few dried or baking beans on top. Bake blind for 10 minutes, until golden. Remove from the oven and leave to cool in the tins. When cold, remove carefully.

Arrange the cherries in the pastry cases. Heat the redcurrant jelly in a small saucepan with the water. Bring to the boil and then sieve and use immediately to brush over the cherries.

Whip the cream until stiff. Put in a piping bag with a star nozzle. Pipe stars on to the middle and around the edges of each amourette.

INGREDIENTS

For the pastry
100 g (4 oz) plain flour, sifted, plus 45–60 ml (3–4 tbsp) to flour board
50 g (2 oz) butter, softened, plus 15 ml (1 tbsp) to grease tins
50 g (2 oz) caster sugar
2 medium egg yolks
Few drops of vanilla essence

For the filling
225 g (8 oz) canned cherries, drained and pitted
60 ml (4 tbsp) redcurrant jelly
15 ml (1 tbsp) water
150 ml (¼ pt) double cream

◆ BRIDESMAIDS' BLOSSOMS ◆

These are little almond biscuits, curled and filled with whipped cream and fruit.

◆ **Preparation** 25–30 minutes ◆ **Cooking** 6–8 minutes ◆ **Makes** 25 biscuits ◆

METHOD

Heat the oven to 400°F (200°C/Gas 6) and grease a baking tray.

Cream the butter and sugar together until light and fluffy. Using a wooden spoon, stir in the flour and almonds and blend well together. Place teaspoonfuls of the mixture, spaced well apart, on the prepared tray and flatten with a fork.

INGREDIENTS

For the biscuit base
75 g (3 oz) butter, softened, plus 5 ml (1 tsp) to grease baking tray
75 g (3 oz) caster sugar
50 g (2 oz) plain flour, sifted
75 g (3 oz) flaked almonds

Continued overleaf

Wedding & celebration tea Clockwise from top: Chocolate pear gâteau (see page 114); Cucumber & mackerel rings (see page 111); Vol-au-vents (see page 110); Bridesmaids' blossoms (see page 113).

For the filling
275 ml (½ pt) double cream
Fresh fruit, prepared and
sliced. Choose from:
    fresh raspberries,
    kiwifruit, skinned and
      sliced
    mandarin orange segments
    fresh strawberries, halved
    cherries, pitted and halved

Pictured opposite page 113

INGREDIENTS

For the cake
150 g (5 oz) plain flour, sifted
25 g (1 oz) cornflour
25 g (1 oz) cocoa powder
6 large eggs
225 g (8 oz) caster sugar
75 g (3 oz) butter, melted and
    cooled, plus 10 ml (2 tsp) to
    grease tins

For the filling
100 g (4 oz) plain chocolate,
    broken into small pieces
2 medium egg yolks
275 ml (½ pt) double cream
2 ripe fresh or canned pears,
    peeled
15 ml (1 tbsp) freshly
    squeezed lemon juice

For the decoration
275 ml (½ pt) double cream
3 large chocolate flake bars,
    broken into long strands
strawberries, sliced (optional)

Pictured opposite page 113

Bake for 6–8 minutes until pale golden. Remove from the oven and leave on the tray for just 1 minute. Remove each biscuit carefully and curl the edges up slightly around a rolling pin. (You will probably need 2 rolling pins to fit all the blossoms on.) Leave on the rolling pins until set, and then remove carefully.

Whip the cream until stiff and put in a piping bag with a star nozzle. Fill each upturned biscuit with piped cream. Arrange raspberries, segments of kiwifruit, mandarin segments, strawberry halves and cherry halves, or any fruit of your choice according to season, on top of the cream and serve immediately.

CHOCOLATE PEAR
♦ GÂTEAU ♦

This is a very decorative gâteau which makes a lovely centrepiece.

♦ **Preparation** 50 minutes, plus 1 hour to chill ♦ **Cooking** 30–35 minutes ♦
♦ **Makes** 25 cm (10 in) gâteau ♦

METHOD

Heat the oven to 375°F (190°C/Gas 5) and grease and line 2 × 25 cm (10 in) round sandwich tins.

Mix together the flour, cornflour and cocoa. Beat the eggs and sugar together in a bowl set over a saucepan of simmering water, beating until the mixture is thick and pale and leaves a trail when the beater is lifted. This will take 3–5 minutes, so do not stop beating until the mixture is really thick. Remove from the heat and beat until cool.

Using a metal spoon, gradually fold in the flour, alternating with the melted butter. Mix carefully to ensure that the ingredients are evenly distributed.

Pour the mixture into the prepared tins and bake for 30–35 minutes until firm. Remove the cake from the oven and turn out on to a wire rack to cool.

For the filling, melt the chocolate in a small bowl set over a saucepan of simmering water. Remove from the heat and beat in the egg yolks, one at a time. Beat in 15 ml (1 tbsp) of the cream. Whip the remaining cream and, with a metal spoon, fold carefully into the chocolate mixture. Chill for 1 hour.

Slice the pears lengthways and sprinkle them with the lemon juice to stop them from turning brown. Spread half the chocolate cream over one of the cakes. Lay two-thirds of the pears over the cream and lay the second cake on top. Spread the remaining chocolate cream on top and arrange the remaining pear slices in a circle in the middle.

To decorate the outside of the cake, whip the cream until stiff. Keep back enough cream to pipe on a trimming of cream around the top, about 45–60 ml (3–4 tbsp), and spread the rest all around the outside of the cake.

Press the flaked chocolate on to the cream. Put the remaining cream into a piping bag with a star nozzle, and pipe all the way around the top edge of the cake to conceal the join between the chocolate cream and the cream. Place slices of strawberries decoratively on the cream, around the cake, if liked.

◆ MERINGUES MARGUERITE ◆

These dainty meringues are sandwiched together with whipped cream and decorated with nuts and chocolate.
It is very important that the bowl used to beat the egg whites is absolutely clean and free from grease.

◆ **Preparation** 45–50 minutes ◆ **Cooking** 4–5 hours ◆ **Makes** 20 meringues ◆

INGREDIENTS

For the meringues
30 ml (2 tbsp) oil, to grease
  baking trays
3 medium egg whites
175 g (6 oz) caster sugar

For the filling and topping
60 ml (4 tbsp) apricot jam
20 ml (1½ tbsp) water
275 ml (½ pt) double cream
150 g (5 oz) chopped toasted
  almonds
50 g (2 oz) plain chocolate
8 g (¼ oz) butter

Pictured opposite page 65

METHOD

Heat the oven to the lowest possible setting, about 225°F (110°C/Gas ¼). Line 2 baking trays with greaseproof paper and brush the paper lightly with oil.

Beat the egg whites until stiff but not dry. Stir in half the sugar and beat hard. Fold in the remaining sugar with a metal spoon.

Place the meringue mixture in a piping bag with a 1.5 cm (½ in) plain nozzle. Pipe 5 cm (2 in) lengths on to the oiled paper (it will make about 40). Place in the oven with the door open and bake for 4–5 hours, until the meringues lift easily off the paper. Leave to cool.

To make the apricot glaze, place the jam and water in a small saucepan and bring to the boil, stirring all the time. Sieve and keep warm. Whip the cream until stiff and pour it into a piping bag with a star nozzle.

Brush the outsides of the meringues all over with the apricot glaze, and then dip them into the almonds, turning to coat completely. Pipe a thick layer of cream on to the flat side of half the meringues and sandwich together with the other halves. Lay the meringues sideways in paper cases, with the middles facing upwards.

Melt the chocolate and butter together in a bowl set over a saucepan of simmering water. Put in a piping bag with a size 1–2 nozzle, or make a little cone from greaseproof paper. Fill with the chocolate butter. Snip the tip off the greaseproof cone if using, and pipe a thin line of chocolate in a zig-zag pattern across the middle of each meringue. Keep in a cool place until needed.

INGREDIENTS
28–30 sponge fingers
100 g (4 oz) caster sugar
8 medium egg yolks
15 g (½ oz) gelatine
30 ml (2 tbsp) water
675 g (1½ lb) fresh raspberries, hulled
700 ml (1¼ pt) double cream

RASPBERRY CHARLOTTE
♦ CAKE ♦

If fresh raspberries are unavailable, frozen ones may be used instead, or fresh strawberries are a nice alternative. This recipe also makes a wonderful dessert for dinner parties.

♦ **Preparation and cooking** 1 hour, plus 6½ hours to chill ♦ **Makes** 12 portions ♦

METHOD

Line the sides of a 1.75 ltr (3 pt) mould with dampened greaseproof paper. Stand a row of the sponge fingers upright around the inside of the mould, with the curved edges of the fingers outermost. Leave the base of the mould free. There should be several fingers left over.

In a large mixing bowl set over a saucepan of gently simmering water, beat the sugar and egg yolks together until pale yellow and thick. Keep beating until the mixture is hot and frothy.

Remove the bowl from the heat and stand in a basin of cold water. Dissolve the gelatine in the water and beat into the egg mixture, continuing to beat until the mixture is cold. Place the bowl in the refrigerator to chill for at least 30 minutes.

Reserve 225 g (8 oz) of the raspberries for decoration and press the rest through a sieve to form a purée. Measure out 425 ml (¾ pt) of the purée into a bowl and chill. Using a metal spoon, fold the remaining purée into the egg yolk mixture.

Whip the cream until stiff and fold 575 ml (1 pt) into the mixture, reserving the rest of the cream in the refrigerator for decoration later. Pour the mixture into the mould and arrange the remaining sponge fingers on the top. If the mixture does not reach the top of the fingers around the edge of the bowl, trim the fingers down to the right level.

Cover the mould with foil and chill in the refrigerator for at least 6 hours. Just before serving, remove the foil and carefully run a knife around the edge of the mould. Place a serving plate over the top and invert both. Give a sharp shake. The charlotte should slide easily out of the mould. If it does not, dip the bowl quickly in hot water to about half its depth and try again. Remove the paper.

Put the remaining cream in a piping bag with a star nozzle. Pipe cream around the edge of the cake and around the base. Decorate the top with the remaining raspberries.

◆ WEDDING RINGS ◆

*These are light, almond-flavoured sponge rings, decorated with cream
and gold icing and with cherries or grapes on top.*

◆ **Preparation** 30–35 minutes ◆ **Cooking** 25–30 minutes ◆ **Makes** 16 rings ◆

METHOD

Heat the oven to 350°F (180°C/Gas 4) and grease and line 2 × 20 cm
(8 in) square tins.

Cream the butter and sugar together until light and fluffy. Add the
eggs, a little at a time, beating hard between each addition. Add the
flour, almonds and almond essence and beat thoroughly.

Turn into the prepared tins and bake for 25–30 minutes until well
risen, golden and firm to the touch. Remove from the oven and turn
out on to a wire rack to cool.

When cold, place the cake on a firm surface and cut out circles with a
7.5 cm (3 in) cutter. Using a 2.5 cm (1 in) cutter, cut out the middle of
the circles to form rings.

Heat the apricot jam and water together in a small saucepan and bring
to the boil, stirring all the time. Sieve, and while still warm, brush the
outsides of the rings to glaze. Roll the rings in the chopped nuts,
turning to coat completely.

Beat the butter until light and fluffy. Add the icing sugar, a little at a
time, beating well after each addition. Add enough of the milk or cream
to make a firm but spreading consistency. Add a few drops of yellow
food colouring to give a strong gold.

Place the butter cream icing in a piping bag with a star nozzle. Pipe
little shells around the outside edge of the top and the edge around the
central hole of each ring.

Whip the cream until stiff. Place in a piping bag with a star nozzle
and pipe scrolls, stars or shells of cream in a circle between the butter
icing. Arrange the cherry or grape halves on the cream.

INGREDIENTS

For the sponge rings
75 g (3 oz) butter, softened,
   plus 10 ml (2 tsp) to grease
   tins
75 g (3 oz) caster sugar
2 medium eggs, beaten
50 g (2 oz) self-raising flour,
   sifted
25 g (1 oz) ground almonds
½ tsp almond essence

For the topping
100 g (4 oz) apricot jam
7.5 ml (1½ tsp) water
75 g (3 oz) chopped toasted
   almonds
100 g (4 oz) butter, softened
175–225 g (6–8 oz) icing
   sugar
15–30 ml (1–2 tbsp) milk or
   single cream
Few drops of yellow food
   colouring
150 ml (¼ pt) double cream
32 cherries or grapes, pitted
   and halved

NOVELTY TEAS

Special teas on a particular theme or to celebrate a seasonal occasion are great fun, and most tea party food can be adapted to suit. Menus follow for a Hallowe'en tea, an ice cream tea and a Valentine's tea, but recipes can be taken from the other chapters in this book and decorated appropriately to suit any event or theme you wish. Fairy cakes, for instance (see page 63) could be iced in light and dark blue for a Boat Race party, and the little pinwheels (see page 112) could be renamed as Catherine wheels for a Guy Fawkes tea. The possibilities are as endless as your imagination.

HALLOWE'EN TEA

Hallowe'en does not have to be just a children's celebration: adults can have fun too. Send invitations on black cards cut in the shape of witches' hats or black cats, and decorate the house with hollowed pumpkin heads with candles burning inside, paper lanterns, autumn leaves and berries.

INGREDIENTS
100 g (4 oz) unsalted butter or
    margarine, softened, plus
    5 ml (1 tsp) to grease tray
100 g (4 oz) caster sugar
1 medium egg, beaten
225 g (8 oz) plain flour, sifted,
    plus 45–60 ml (3–4 tbsp) to
    flour board
15 g (½ oz) cocoa powder
50 g (2 oz) glacé cherries,
    chopped

♦ ABRACADABRAS ♦

Two layers of light and dark sponge are rolled up together and then sliced and baked.

♦ **Preparation** 15–20 minutes, plus 30 minutes to chill ♦ **Cooking** 15–20 minutes ♦
♦ **Makes** 14–16 cakes ♦

METHOD
Cream the fat and sugar together until light and fluffy. Beat in the egg, and then mix the flour in well to form a firm dough.

Divide the dough in half. Work the cocoa powder into one portion and the chopped cherries into the other.

Roll out each portion on a floured board to a rectangle of about

23 × 15 cm (9 × 6 in). Carefully press the chocolate rectangle on top of the other. Roll up carefully, wrap in cling film, and chill for about 30 minutes.

Heat the oven to 350°F (180°C/Gas 4) and grease a baking tray. Using a very sharp knife, trim the edges of the roll and then cut it into 14–16 little pinwheels.

Place the pinwheels on the prepared tray and bake for 15–20 minutes until lightly browned. Remove from the oven and transfer to a wire rack to cool.

◆ ELFIN DIP ◆

Serve this savoury dip with tortilla chips, potato crisps and wide strips of green pepper, courgettes or celery. Alternatively, it can be served as a topping for baked potatoes.

◆ **Preparation and cooking** 15–20 minutes ◆ **Makes** About 275 ml ($\frac{1}{2}$ pt) dip ◆

METHOD

Cut the bacon into thin strips. Fry quickly in the oil or butter until golden brown and crisp. Drain on a paper towel and leave to cool.

Mix the sweetcorn with the mayonnaise, chives and black pepper. Add the bacon and mix well.

To serve, place in a serving bowl and stand the bowl on a larger serving plate. Arrange tortilla chips, crisps and strips of vegetables around the dip.

INGREDIENTS

50 g (2 oz) rashers of streaky bacon, with rind and bones removed

15 ml (1 tbsp) oil or butter, to fry bacon

300 g (11 oz) can of sweetcorn, drained

40 ml (2$\frac{1}{2}$ tbsp) mayonnaise

5 ml (1 tsp) fresh or freeze-dried chives

Freshly ground black pepper

◆ FAIRY FLYAWAYS ◆

These are little almond biscuits with a chocolate base.

◆ **Preparation** 20–25 minutes ◆ **Cooking** 25–30 minutes ◆ **Makes** 18–20 biscuits ◆

METHOD

Heat the oven to 225°F (110°C/Gas $\frac{1}{4}$) and grease and line 2 large baking trays.

Beat the egg whites until stiff but not dry. Beat in half the icing sugar. Using a metal spoon, fold in the remaining sugar and the ground and chopped almonds.

Spoon the mixture on to the prepared trays in circles about 6 cm (2$\frac{1}{2}$ in) in diameter. Bake for 25–30 minutes until firm but not browned. Remove from the oven and transfer carefully to a wire rack to cool.

Melt the chocolate and butter together in a bowl set over a saucepan of gently simmering water. Spread on to the underside of each flyaway and leave, chocolate side up, to dry.

INGREDIENTS

10 ml (2 tsp) margarine, to grease baking trays

2 medium egg whites

50 g (2 oz) icing sugar

50 g (2 oz) ground almonds

50 g (2 oz) finely chopped almonds

50 g (2 oz) plain chocolate

15 g ($\frac{1}{2}$ oz) butter

INGREDIENTS

100 g (4 oz) butter, softened,
    plus 5 ml (1 tsp) to grease
    tin
75 g (3 oz) demerara sugar
1 medium egg yolk
175 g (6 oz) plain flour, sifted
½ tsp ground cinnamon
½ tsp ground mixed spice
75 g (3 oz) raisins, chopped
25 g (1 oz) chopped walnuts
9 glacé cherries, halved

◆ SPICY SPELLS ◆

These are spicy walnut and raisin squares, topped with glacé cherries.

◆ **Preparation** 15–20 minutes ◆ **Cooking** 30 minutes ◆ **Makes** 18 pieces ◆

METHOD

Heat the oven to 325°F (170°C/Gas 3) and grease and line a 28 × 18 cm (11 × 7 in) shallow tin.

Cream the butter and sugar together until light and fluffy. Beat in the egg yolk. Using a wooden spoon, mix in the flour, spices, raisins and nuts. Mix thoroughly until well blended. The mixture should be quite crumbly.

Turn into the prepared tin and press down with a palette knife. Smooth the top and mark into 18 squares. Press a cherry half into the middle of each square.

Bake for 30 minutes until pale golden. Remove from the oven and cut through the squares while still hot. Leave to cool completely in the tin before turning out.

INGREDIENTS

3 slices of white bread
3 slices of brown bread
30 g (1½ oz) butter, softened
75 g (3 oz) Cheddar cheese,
    sliced thinly
Lettuce leaves, shredded
1 red pepper, sliced thinly
2 slices of ham
1 punnet of mustard and cress

◆ WITCHES' WEDGES ◆

These colourful double-decker sandwiches are filled with cheese, red pepper, ham and lettuce. Other salad ingredients can be added or substituted as liked. Garnish with neat bunches of mustard and cress.

◆ **Preparation** 10–15 minutes ◆ **Makes** 8 small sandwiches ◆

METHOD

Spread the slices of bread with the butter. Take 1 white slice and 1 brown slice, and lay some sliced cheese and a few pieces of shredded lettuce on each. Add a few slices of red pepper.

Placing the buttered side downwards, lay a brown slice of bread on top of the white base and a white slice on top of the brown. Butter the upper sides of the bread.

Place a slice of ham on each and scatter with mustard and cress. Place the last white slice on top of the brown middle and the last brown slice on top of the white middle. Press gently together.

Carefully trim off the crusts and cut each into 4 wedges. Arrange on a serving plate.

✦ WITCH'S HAT ✦

This is a plain or chocolate sponge, shaped into a cone and covered in black sugar paste to form a witch's black hat.

✦ **Preparation** About 1½ hours ✦ **Cooking** 20–25 minutes ✦ **Makes** 12–16 portions ✦

METHOD

Heat the oven to 350°F (180°C/Gas 4). Grease and line 2 × 15 cm (6 in) round sandwich tins and grease a 575 ml (1 pt) ovenproof pudding basin well.

Cream the fat and sugar together until light and fluffy. Add the eggs one at a time, beating well after each egg, and adding 15 ml (1 tbsp) of the flour with the second and third eggs. Using a metal spoon, fold in the rest of the flour (or flour and cocoa) and mix well.

Divide the mixture between the tins and the basin and bake for 20–25 minutes. Test the mixture in the basin after 20 minutes, as it is likely to cook more quickly than in the tins. Remove from the oven, leave for a few minutes in the containers and then turn out the cakes on to a wire rack to cool.

While the cake is cooling, make the butter icing. Beat the butter until light and fluffy. Add the icing sugar a little at a time, beating well after each addition. Add enough of the milk or cream to give a firm but spreading consistency.

When the cake is quite cold, place one of the sandwich cakes on a wide cake board. There must be enough room around the cake for the brim of the hat to sit. Cover the cake with a layer of butter icing and place the other sandwich cake on top. Cover that with butter icing and place the cake cooked in the basin upside-down on top.

Cut and shape the cake into a cone, spreading butter icing wherever the cake needs to be stuck together. Use pieces cut from the base to build up the height. When the cone is built, cover the entire cone with a thin layer of butter icing.

Make the sugar paste. Place the icing sugar in a bowl and make a well in the middle. Add all the other ingredients except the colouring, adding enough glucose to make a pliable but not sticky paste. Mix thoroughly with a fork, and then knead the paste with your hands until smooth and even. If the paste is too wet, add a little extra icing sugar.

Keep back a small quantity of the sugar paste to use later for decoration, about a 4 cm (1½ in) diameter ball. Mix the rest with black food colouring, kneading well to make quite sure that there are no streaks. Make sure that your hands are cool and not sticky.

Roll out the black sugar paste quite thickly on a lightly sugared board. Cover the outside of the cone with a layer of the paste, using

INGREDIENTS

For the cake
175 g (6 oz) margarine or butter, softened, plus 15 ml (1 tbsp) to grease tins and basin
175 g (6 oz) caster sugar
3 medium eggs
225 g (8 oz) self-raising flour, sifted, *OR* 200 g (7 oz) self-raising flour, sifted, mixed with 25 g (1 oz) cocoa powder

For the butter icing
100 g (4 oz) butter, softened
175–225 g (6–8 oz) icing sugar
15–30 ml (1–2 tbsp) milk or single cream

For the sugar paste
675 g (1½ lb) icing sugar, plus 25–50 g (1–2 oz) to sugar board
65–75 ml (4½–5 tbsp) liquid glucose
7.5 ml (1½ tsp) glycerine
2 small egg whites, lightly beaten
15–20 ml (3–4 tsp) freshly squeezed lemon juice
Black and yellow food colouring

Continued overleaf

about three-quarters, dampening the edges wherever it has to be joined together. Use your hands to form and smooth the paste (it is a little like working with putty!).

Cut a brim out of the remaining quarter of black paste to sit around the hat and join carefully to the paste at the base of the cone. Add some yellow food colouring to the reserved piece of sugar paste and knead well. On a lightly sugared board, roll out quite thickly and then cut out star and moon shapes to decorate the hat. Dampen one side of each shape and press on the hat.

To cut the hat into portions, first slice down through the middle. Slice each half lengthways into 6–8 pieces.

♦ WIZARDS' WANDS ♦

The wands are cheese straws sandwiched together with a little cream cheese, with a star cut from a slice of carrot fixed at one end.

♦ **Preparation** 25–30 minutes ♦ **Cooking** 15–20 minutes ♦ **Makes** 14–16 wands ♦

INGREDIENTS

65 g (2½ oz) plain flour, sifted, plus 45–60 ml (3–4 tbsp) to flour board
Pinch of salt
Pinch of cayenne pepper
50 g (2 oz) Parmesan cheese, grated
50 g (2 oz) butter, softened, plus 5 ml (1 tsp) to grease baking tray
25 g (1 oz) mature Cheddar cheese, grated
1 medium egg yolk, beaten
1–2 fat carrots
50 g (2 oz) cream cheese, softened

METHOD

Heat the oven to 325°F (170°C/Gas 3) and grease a large baking tray.

Mix together the flour, salt, cayenne and Parmesan cheese in a bowl. Rub or cut in the butter until the mixture resembles moist breadcrumbs. Mix in the grated Cheddar cheese.

Add the egg yolk and bind together with a fork to form a stiff dough. If too stiff, add a little cold water.

Roll out the dough thinly on a floured board and cut into strips, about 10 cm (4 in) long and 1 cm (½ in) wide. Place the strips carefully on the prepared tray.

Bake for 15–20 minutes until light golden and crisp. Remove from the oven and leave to cool for 2–3 minutes on the tray before transferring carefully to a wire rack to cool completely.

Peel the carrots and slice into very thin circles. Cut a star from each slice. Spread a little cream cheese on half the cheese biscuits. Lay a carrot star at one end so that it sticks out like the star on the end of a wand. Spread a little cream cheese on one end of each of the remaining biscuits where the carrot star will lie, and sandwich the biscuits together. The star should be held in place by the biscuits and cream cheese.

ICE CREAM TEA

On a hot midsummer afternoon, an ice cream tea party is an unusual and exciting way to entertain. Make sure that your refrigerator and freezer have plenty of space to store the chilled and frozen goodies, and that you have plenty of ice for cold drinks and iced tea. Of course the food does not have to be only ice cream. Choose sandwiches and savouries from the other chapters of this book, preparing them ahead and keeping them cool by covering with a damp serviette or cloth. Store them in the refrigerator until required.

♦ BAKED ALASKA ♦

This is often served as a dessert for dinner parties, but it is such an impressive and delicious creation that it would be a shame to leave it out of an ice cream tea.

♦ **Preparation** 30 minutes ♦ **Cooking** 20–25 minutes ♦ **Makes** 8–10 portions ♦

METHOD

Place the ice cream on to a piece of foil and mould it gently to fit a 20 cm (8 in) round sandwich tin. Cover it with the foil and freeze.

Heat the oven to 350°F (180°C/Gas 4) and grease 2 × 20 cm (8 in) round sandwich tins. Mix together the extra 15 ml (1 tbsp) flour with the extra 15 ml (1 tbsp) sugar, and dust the tins with the mixture. Tap out any surplus.

Beat the egg yolks and vanilla together in a medium bowl until thick and creamy. Keep back 60 ml (4 tbsp) of the sugar and add the rest to the mixture. Beat thoroughly.

Beat the egg whites in a dry, grease-free bowl until stiff. Add the reserved sugar and beat well. With a metal spoon, fold the egg whites into the yolks and make sure that they are well blended.

Fold the flour, baking powder and salt into the mixture. Pour evenly into the prepared tins and bake for 20–25 minutes until a skewer comes out clean. Remove from the oven and turn out carefully on to a wire rack to cool. When cool, spread one cake with the jam. Place the other cake on top.

Heat the oven to 450°F (230°C/Gas 8). Beat the egg whites and salt together until stiff. Add the sugar, a little at a time, beating continuously. Continue beating until the meringue is stiff and glossy.

Place the cake on a flat baking tray. Take the foil off the ice cream and place it quickly on top of the cake. Cover the outside of the cake and ice cream completely with the meringue.

Place the baking tray in the middle of the oven and bake for 3–4 minutes only until pale and golden. Serve immediately.

INGREDIENTS

For the cake
1.25 ltr (2 pt) vanilla ice cream, slightly softened
10 ml (2 tsp) margarine, to grease tins
4 medium eggs, separated
5 ml (1 tsp) vanilla essence
175 g (6 oz) caster sugar, plus 15 ml (1 tbsp) to dust tins
75 g (3 oz) plain flour, sifted, plus 15 ml (1 tbsp) to dust tins
5 ml (1 tsp) baking powder
Pinch of salt
225 g (8 oz) apricot or raspberry jam

For the meringue
6 medium egg whites
Pinch of salt
175 g (6 oz) caster sugar

BLACKCURRANT ICE CREAM
♦ WITH RASPBERRY SAUCE ♦

This sauce can also be made with fresh strawberries, and is delicious with vanilla ice cream. You will need a liquidizer or blender to make the sauce.

♦ **Preparation** 20–25 minutes, plus $2\frac{1}{2}$–3 hours to freeze ♦ **Makes** 4 portions ♦

INGREDIENTS

For the ice cream
450 g (1 lb) blackcurrants, with stalks removed
225 g (8 oz) icing sugar
Juice of $\frac{1}{2}$ lemon
275 ml ($\frac{1}{2}$ pt) double cream

For the sauce
450 g (1 lb) fresh raspberries, hulled
Juice of 2 lemons
175 g (6 oz) caster sugar

METHOD

Using a wooden spoon, press the blackcurrants through a nylon sieve. Retain the juice and discard the skins.

To the juice, add the icing sugar and lemon juice and mix well. Beat the cream until thick and fold into the mixture with a metal spoon.

Pour the blackcurrant cream into a large freezeproof plastic container, leaving 1 cm ($\frac{1}{2}$ in) space at the top. Cover and freeze until firm, about $2\frac{1}{2}$–3 hours.

For the sauce, place the fruit, lemon juice and sugar in a liquidizer and blend well. Pour over scoops of the ice cream and serve.

♦ FROSTED CHOCOLATE ♦

You will need a liquidizer or cocktail shaker for this recipe.

♦ **Preparation** 3–4 minutes ♦ **Makes** 4 glasses ♦

INGREDIENTS

60 ml (4 tbsp) drinking chocolate powder
60 ml (4 tbsp) hot water
575 ml (1 pt) milk
150 ml ($\frac{1}{4}$ pt) vanilla ice cream
Ice cubes or crushed ice

METHOD

Dissolve the chocolate powder in the hot water. Blend with the milk and ice cream in a cocktail shaker or liquidizer. Pour into glasses over ice cubes or crushed ice and drink immediately.

♦ ICE CREAM MERINGUES ♦

For variety, if liked, these meringue shells may have a little food colouring added to the egg whites during preparation, and different colour ice cream may be used.

♦ **Preparation** 10–15 minutes ♦ **Cooking** 4–5 hours ♦ **Makes** 5–6 meringues ♦

INGREDIENTS

For the meringues
15 ml (1 tbsp) oil, to grease paper
2 medium egg whites
Pinch of salt
100 g (4 oz) caster sugar

For the filling
About 75 ml (3 fl oz) strawberry or raspberry ripple ice cream
10–12 pistachio nuts, chopped

METHOD

Heat the oven to the lowest possible heat, 225°F (110°C/Gas $\frac{1}{4}$). Line 2 large baking trays with greaseproof paper and brush lightly with oil.

Beat the egg whites with the salt until they are stiff and dry and peak when the beater is lifted. Mix in half the sugar, beating thoroughly. Fold in the rest of the sugar with a metal spoon.

Place spoonfuls of the mixture on the oiled paper, about 10 or 12. Place in the oven and bake for 4–5 hours. Transfer carefully to an airtight container until needed.

Just before serving, sandwich the meringues together with scoops of the ice cream. Place in paper cases and scatter a few nuts over the filling.

◆ ICE CREAM SANDWICH ◆

This is a Victoria sponge cake filled with jam and ice cream, and topped with cream and fruit.

◆ **Preparation** 1 hour ◆ **Cooking** 20–25 minutes ◆ **Makes** 18 cm (7 in) round tin ◆

METHOD

Heat the oven to 350°F (180°C/Gas 4) and grease and line 2 × 18 cm (7 in) round sandwich tins.

Cream the fat and sugar together until light and fluffy. Beat in the eggs, a little at a time, beating well and adding 15 ml (1 tbsp) of the flour between each addition. Beat very thoroughly.

Fold in the remaining flour with a metal spoon. Finally, stir in the boiling water and mix well. Pour the mixture into the prepared tins, and bake for 20–25 minutes until the cake is lightly browned and springs back when pressed lightly with a finger.

Remove from the oven and turn out on to a wire rack to cool. When cold, place one of the cakes on a plate or serving tray. Spread with a layer of jam. Whip the cream until stiff and put in a piping bag.

Carefully slice the ice cream and place a layer of slices all over the jam. Spread the underside of the other sponge cake with jam and place on top of the ice cream.

Quickly pipe the cream over the top of the cake and arrange the raspberries decoratively on top. Serve immediately.

INGREDIENTS

For the cake
100 g (4 oz) margarine or butter, softened, plus 10 ml (2 tsp) to grease tins
100 g (4 oz) caster sugar
2 medium eggs, beaten
100 g (4 oz) self-raising flour, sifted
15 ml (1 tbsp) boiling water

For the filling and topping
45–60 ml (3–4 tbsp) raspberry jam
150 ml ($\frac{1}{4}$ pt) double cream
275 ml ($\frac{1}{2}$ pt) vanilla ice cream
About 20 fresh raspberries, hulled

◆ STRAWBERRY FLOAT ◆

Cubes of ice cream and fresh strawberries float on top of clear green soda water in this refreshing drink.

◆ **Preparation** 10 minutes ◆ **Makes** 6 glasses ◆

METHOD

Pour the lime cordial into 6 individual glasses and pour in the soda water, leaving room for the fruit and ice cream. Add a few strawberries to each, halving the larger ones. Float the cubes of ice cream on the top and serve immediately.

INGREDIENTS

90 ml (6 tbsp) lime cordial, chilled
2 ltr ($3\frac{1}{2}$ pt) bottle of soda water, chilled
About 30 strawberries, depending on size
275 ml ($\frac{1}{2}$ pt) vanilla ice cream, cut into cubes

VALENTINE'S TEA

A Valentine's tea party can be for a couple alone or for friends and family. Send out invitations on red and white heart-shaped cards and decorate the room with fresh red and white flowers. Arrange a vase of red roses on the table and give the guests a rose or carnation to wear. The recipes suggested here are adaptations of other recipes and are designed to give a romantic and slightly exotic feel to the party. Individual cooks will be able to invent all sorts of other suitable items.

INGREDIENTS

3 slices of wholewheat bread
25 g (1 oz) butter, softened
100 g (4 oz) smoked salmon
50 g (2 oz) cream cheese
½ tsp freshly squeezed lemon juice
Salt and freshly ground black pepper
2.5–4 cm (1–1½ in) piece of cucumber, skinned
1 punnet of mustard and cress, to decorate canapés

Pictured opposite page 128

◆ CANAPÉS D'AMOUR ◆

Small crustless slices of toast are topped with a creamy mixture of salmon, cream cheese and cucumber. A simple, but attractive, alternative is to cut out hearts of smoked salmon and serve them as canapé toppings on bread.

◆ **Preparation** 15–20 minutes ◆ **Makes** 12 canapés ◆

METHOD

Toast the bread lightly and spread with the butter. Trim off the crusts.

Place the salmon, cream cheese, lemon juice, salt and black pepper in a liquidizer and blend well together. Dice the cucumber finely and stir into the salmon mixture.

Using a heart-shaped cutter, cut out hearts from the toast. (Alternatively, cut each slice into 4 squares or triangles.) Pile the salmon mixture on to the toast. Place a tiny bunch of mustard and cress on top of each, to decorate.

INGREDIENTS

5 ml (1 tsp) margarine, to grease baking tray
85 g (3½ oz) cocoa powder
25 g (1 oz) finely chopped walnuts
75 g (3 oz) ground almonds
50 g (2 oz) icing sugar, plus extra to sugar hands
Few drops of vanilla flavouring
1 medium egg, separated
8–9 glacé cherries, halved

◆ CHOCOLATE VALENTINES ◆

These are little chocolate petits fours.

◆ **Preparation** 15 minutes ◆ **Cooking** 15 minutes ◆ **Makes** 16 petits fours ◆

METHOD

Heat the oven to 250°F (130°C/Gas ½) and grease a baking tray.

Mix together the cocoa, walnuts, almonds, icing sugar and vanilla in a bowl. Lightly beat the egg white until stiff and add enough to the dry ingredients to form a stiff paste.

Knead the mixture together with sugared hands until smooth. Divide into about 16 pieces. Roll between the palms of the hands to form into smooth balls.

Press your little finger into the middle of each ball to make a hollow large enough to hold a glacé cherry half. Beat the egg yolk and brush over the balls to glaze, and then press a glacé cherry half into each.

Place on the prepared tray and bake in the middle of the oven for about 15 minutes. Take out and transfer carefully to a wire rack to cool.

♦ CREAM CHEESE HEARTS ♦

These are heart-shaped sandwiches of white bread, filled with cream cheese and decorated with tiny red pepper hearts.

♦ **Preparation** 20–25 minutes ♦ **Makes** 6–8 small sandwiches ♦

INGREDIENTS
1 red pepper
50 g (2 oz) cream cheese
Salt and freshly ground black
  pepper
4 slices of white bread
35 g (1½ oz) butter, softened

Pictured opposite page 128

METHOD
Chop two-thirds of the red pepper into small pieces and mix with the cream cheese and seasoning.

Spread the bread with the butter and spread the cream cheese mixture on to 2 slices, keeping a little cream cheese back for decoration. Press the other slices of bread on top. Trim off the crusts and cut out 3–4 hearts from each sandwich with a heart-shaped cutter.

Cut the remaining red pepper into tiny heart shapes with a sharp knife and use to decorate the little sandwiches. Put the remaining cream cheese in a piping bag with a size 1–2 nozzle and pipe a larger heart shape around each red pepper heart.

♦ CUPID COFFEE CAKE ♦

The best way to crumble the biscuits for this is to place them in a plastic bag and roll firmly with a rolling pin.

♦ **Preparation and cooking** 15 minutes, plus 1 hour to chill ♦ **Makes** 8 portions ♦

INGREDIENTS
100 g (4 oz) butter, plus 5 ml
  (1 tsp) to grease tin
50 g (2 oz) soft brown sugar
30 ml (2 tbsp) syrup
30 ml (2 tbsp) instant coffee
10 ml (2 tsp) hot water
225 g (8 oz) digestive biscuits,
  crumbled finely
8 walnut or almond halves

METHOD
Grease and line an 18 cm (7 in) round sandwich tin.

Melt together the butter, sugar and syrup in a saucepan over a gentle heat. Dissolve the coffee in the water and add with the biscuits to the pan. Blend well together. Press into the prepared tin and smooth the top with a palette knife.

Arrange the walnut or almond halves around the edge of the cake and press into the mixture. Chill for at least 1 hour. Cut into 8 portions before turning out.

INGREDIENTS

65 g (2½ oz) plain flour, sifted,
  plus 45–60 ml (3–4 tbsp) to
  flour board and fingers
50 g (2 oz) Parmesan cheese,
  grated
Pinch of salt
Pinch of cayenne pepper
50 g (2 oz) butter, softened,
  plus 5 ml (1 tsp) to grease
  baking tray
25 g (1 oz) mature Cheddar
  cheese, grated
1 medium egg yolk, beaten
5–10 ml (1–2 tsp) milk

Pictured opposite

◆ LOVERS' KNOTS ◆

*These are made from the same cheese-straw mixture used for Wizards'
wands (see page 122), but the dough is more soft and pliable so that it
can be rolled and tied.*

◆ **Preparation** 15 minutes ◆ **Cooking** 15–20 minutes ◆ **Makes** 10–12 knots ◆

METHOD

Heat the oven to 325°F (170°C/Gas 3) and grease a large baking tray.

Mix together the flour, Parmesan cheese, salt and cayenne pepper in a
bowl. Rub or cut in the butter until the mixture resembles moist
breadcrumbs. Mix in the Cheddar cheese.

Add the egg yolk and bind together with a fork to make a soft
dough. Add a little milk, just enough to make the dough pliable.
Mix in well.

Divide the dough into 10–12 pieces and, on a floured board and with
floured fingers, roll out each piece of dough to a thin sausage, about
25.5 cm (10 in) long. Very carefully, knot one end through the other
and place on the prepared tray.

Bake for 15–20 minutes until light golden and crisp. Remove from
the oven and leave to cool on the tray for 2–3 minutes before
transferring carefully to a wire rack to cool completely.

INGREDIENTS

For the meringues
15 ml (1 tbsp) oil, to grease
4 medium egg whites
Pinch of salt
225 g (8 oz) caster sugar
100 g (4 oz) finely chopped
  hazelnuts or almonds

For the filling
50 g (2 oz) crushed pineapple,
  drained
15–30 ml (1–2 tbsp) brandy
150 ml (¼ pt) double cream
Few pineapple pieces or
  kiwifruit slices, to decorate

Pictured opposite

Continued on page 129

◆ MERINGUE KISSES ◆

*These are heart-shaped meringues filled with brandy-soaked pineapple
and whipped cream.*

◆ **Preparation** 30 minutes ◆ **Cooking** 30 minutes ◆ **Makes** 10 meringues ◆

METHOD

Soak the pineapple for the filling in the brandy for 1 hour.

Heat the oven to 300°F (150°C/Gas 2). Line 2 baking trays with
greaseproof paper and brush lightly with oil.

Beat the egg whites with the salt until stiff and then beat in half the
sugar. Continue beating for 1–2 minutes. With a metal spoon, fold in
the remaining sugar and the nuts. Place the mixture in a piping bag
with a 1 cm (½ in) star nozzle.

Pipe the meringue mixture into 10 heart shapes on the oiled paper,
each measuring about 6.5 cm (2½ in) in width and 5 cm (2 in) from the
inside of the indentation at the top of the heart to the point at the
bottom. Build up the sides and leave the centre hollow.

Valentine's tea Clockwise from top right: Lovers' knots (see page 128); Meringue kisses (see page 128); Venus dream cake (see page 130); Canapés d'amour (see page 126); Cream cheese hearts (see page 127).

Bake for 30 minutes until they are pale cream in colour and can be easily removed from the tray. Remove from the oven and leave to cool on the trays.

Drain the pineapple, reserving the juice and brandy. Whip the cream until stiff. Gradually add enough of the brandy and juice for the cream to still be stiff and hold its shape. Fold in the pineapple and blend well.

Pile the filling into the meringue hearts and decorate, if liked, with pineapple pieces. If using kiwifruit to decorate, peel and slice the fruit first and cut each slice into 3 fan-shaped segments. Arrange the segments over the hearts, if using.

◆ SWEETHEARTS ◆

These are little tartlets filled with black cherry jam, topped with cream and flavoured with kirsch and grated chocolate.

◆ **Preparation** 20–25 minutes, plus 25 minutes for pastry ◆ **Cooking** 15–20 minutes ◆
◆ **Makes** 12 tarts ◆

METHOD

Make the pastry as on page 138 and chill for 15 minutes.

Heat the oven to 400°F (200°C/Gas 6) and grease 12 patty tins.

Roll out the pastry thinly on a floured board and cut out circles using a 9 cm (3½ in) cutter. Use to line the prepared tins. Place a circle of greaseproof paper in the middle of each and place a few dried or baking beans on top.

Bake the tarts blind for 15–20 minutes until light golden. Remove from the oven, take out the beans and paper and leave to cool in the tins. Remove carefully. Place a spoonful of jam in the base of each.

Whip the cream until stiff and gradually add the kirsch, mixing carefully so that it is well blended into the cream. Using a metal spoon, fold in the chocolate and sugar.

Spoon the cream into the pastry cases. Sprinkle a little grated chocolate over the tops to decorate.

INGREDIENTS

½ quantity rich shortcrust pastry, using 100 g (4 oz) flour (see page 138)
10 ml (2 tsp) margarine, to grease tins
30–45 ml (2–3 tbsp) flour, to flour board
45–60 ml (3–4 tbsp) black cherry jam
150 ml (¼ pt) double cream
15 ml (1 tbsp) kirsch
50 g (2 oz) chocolate, grated, plus 15–30 ml (1–2 tbsp) extra, to decorate tarts
50 g (2 oz) caster sugar

Afternoon tea Clockwise from left: Victoria sponge (see page 82); Teacakes (see page 51); Cheese & cucumber sandwiches (see page 38); Sardine & tomato sandwiches (see page 41); Macaroons (see page 56).

INGREDIENTS

For the pastry cases
¼ quantity puff pastry, using
   100 g (4 oz) flour (see page
   137)
5 ml (1 tsp) margarine, to
   grease baking tray
45–60 ml (3–4 tbsp) flour, to
   flour board
1 medium egg, beaten, to
   glaze pastry

For the filling
75 g (3 oz) cream cheese
2 small sticks of celery,
   chopped finely
100 g (4 oz) cooked white
   chicken meat, chopped
Salt and freshly ground black
   pepper
Pinch of cayenne pepper

◆ VALENTINE VOL-AU-VENTS ◆

*These are puff pastry cases filled with a mixture of white chicken meat,
cream cheese and celery. Make the cases whatever shape and size you
like. Garnish with sprigs of watercress or parsley.*

◆ **Preparation** 30 minutes, plus 4 hours for pastry ◆ **Cooking** 10–12 minutes ◆
◆ **Makes** 15–20 vol-au-vents, depending on the size of cutter ◆

METHOD

Make the pastry as on page 137 and chill for 30 minutes.
   Heat the oven to 450°F (230°C/Gas 8) and grease a baking tray.
   Roll out the pastry thinly on a floured board. Using a cutter of your
choice, dipped in flour, press firmly through the pastry to cut out
shapes. Place the pastry shapes on the prepared tray and brush with the
beaten egg. Using a smaller cutter, also dipped in flour, press a circle
into the middle of each, pressing the cutter about half-way down into
the pastry.
   Bake for 10–12 minutes until golden. Remove from the oven and
transfer carefully to a wire rack to cool. Remove the lids and pull out
any damp pastry from the middles.
   Beat the cream cheese until fluffy. Mix in the celery and then the
chicken. Add the salt, pepper and cayenne.
   Carefully spoon the mixture into the pastry cases. Replace the lids
and arrange on a serving dish.

INGREDIENTS

For the cake
5 ml (1 tsp) margarine, to
   grease tin
2 medium eggs
100 g (4 oz) caster sugar
100 g (4 oz) plain flour, sifted
30 ml (2 tbsp) hot water

◆ VENUS DREAM CAKE ◆

*This is a light sponge cake, filled with pineapple and cream and
decorated with cream, pineapple and kiwifruit. Other fruit such as
grapes, mandarins, oranges, peaches, strawberries or raspberries can also
be used. If liked, smaller cakes can be cut from the sponge and
decorated individually.*

◆ **Preparation** ¾–1 hour ◆ **Cooking** 12–15 minutes ◆
◆ **Makes** 28 cm (11 in) cake or 8 small cakes ◆

METHOD

Heat the oven to 425°F (220°C/Gas 7) and grease and line a 28 × 18 cm
(11 × 7 in) Swiss roll tin.
   Beat the eggs and sugar together in a bowl set over a saucepan of
gently simmering water, until the mixture is very thick and leaves a trail
when the beater is lifted (this takes about 6–8 minutes). Remove from
the heat.

Add the flour and hot water and mix gently with a metal spoon. Turn into the prepared tin and bake for 12–15 minutes until pale golden and firm. Remove from the oven and turn out on to a wire rack to cool. Remove the lining paper.

Trim the edges of the cake and cut in half, lengthways. Mix together the juice from the can of pineapple and the sherry, and pour over both halves of the cake. If making individual cakes, cut each half into 8 slices. Place one half or 8 little slices of the cake on a serving dish or tray.

Whip the cream until stiff. Keep back about 45 ml (3 tbsp) and place the rest in a piping bag with a star nozzle. Pipe ribbons of cream on to the cake(s), leaving a little in the bag for later. Cut the pineapple rings in half and arrange a layer on top of the cream. Place the second cake(s) carefully on top.

Use a little of the reserved cream to spread a thin layer of cream over the top of the cake(s). Place 7–8 pineapple halves along the middle, and lay a slice of kiwifruit in between each pineapple.

Pipe shells of the remaining cream in the piping bag all along the edges of the cake(s), and arrange the grape halves, if using, neatly along the edges.

For the filling and topping
394 g (14 oz) can of pineapple rings, drained and halved, reserving the juice
45 ml (3 tbsp) sweet or medium-sweet sherry
275 ml (½ pt) double cream
2 kiwifruit, peeled and sliced neatly
6–8 black grapes, halved and pipped (optional)

Pictured opposite page 128

JAMS & PRESERVES

Home-made jams and preserves are wonderful on fresh bread, scones and toast at tea time, and far superior to the bought varieties. They are also a good way of using up perishable fruit. Recipes in this chapter include a delicious traditional blackberry and apple jam, a creamy lemon curd, and a more unusual pineapple and peach jam. There is even a recipe for a rich mincemeat, lovely in Christmas pies and tarts.

There are a few golden rules for successful jam making. Do not use half-ripe, over-ripe or blemished fruit, and use white preserving sugar rather than brown, or the flavour of the fruit may be overpowered. Choose a preserving pan (preferably of aluminium or stainless steel) which is large enough—it should only be half full when the fruit and sugar are mixed together. Finally, make sure that you pour the jam into jars which are clean, dry and warm.

INGREDIENTS
1.8 kg (4 lb) apricots, stoned
    and sliced
90 ml (3½ fl oz) lemon juice
275 ml (½ pt) water
2.7 kg (6 lb) preserving sugar
450 g (1 lb) split almonds
1 bottle of pectin

♦ APRICOT & ALMOND JAM ♦

This is one of my favourite jams, delicious with hot rolls, croissants and toast.

♦ **Preparation and cooking** 25–30 minutes ♦ **Makes** 4.5 kg (10 lb) jam ♦

METHOD

Place the prepared apricots in a preserving pan with the lemon juice and water. Cover, bring to the boil and simmer gently for 15–20 minutes or until the fruit is tender.

Lower the heat, add the sugar and almonds and stir until the sugar has dissolved. Bring to the boil and boil rapidly for 1 minute, stirring the mixture occasionally.

Remove from the heat and stir in the pectin. Blend thoroughly. Leave to cool in the pan for 10 minutes and then pour into clean, dry, warm jars. Place wax discs on top of each pot, cover, seal and label.

◆ BLACKBERRY & APPLE JAM ◆

This is a wonderfully cheap jam if you have windfall apples to use up and can find wild blackberries. Pick the berries over carefully before using to remove any bad or unripe fruit.

◆ **Preparation and cooking** 1 hour ◆ **Makes** 2.7 kg (6 lb) jam ◆

METHOD

Quarter the peeled and cored apples. Place in a preserving pan with the water. Bring to the boil and simmer gently for about 15 minutes until tender. Add the blackberries and continue simmering for a further 10–15 minutes.

Remove from the heat and stir the sugar in well. Stir over a low heat until the sugar dissolves, about 15–20 minutes; then bring to the boil and boil hard for 10–15 minutes, stirring occasionally. To test for setting point, remove from the heat and spoon a little jam on to a cold plate or saucer and allow to cool. The jam is ready if a skin forms and wrinkles when pushed with a finger.

When ready, remove from the heat and leave to cool for 5–10 minutes. Pour the jam into clean, dry, warm jars. Place wax discs on top of each jar, cover, seal and label.

INGREDIENTS

900 g (2 lb) sour apples, prepared (weight after peeling and coring)
275 ml (½ pt) water
900 g (2 lb) blackberries, hulled
425 ml (¾ pt) preserving sugar

◆ LEMON CURD ◆

This is delicious spread on bread, muffins and toast and can be used to fill the lemon tarts on page 66. It will keep for 3–4 months if stored in a refrigerator. Otherwise, eat within 3–4 days.

◆ **Preparation and cooking** 25–30 minutes ◆ **Makes** 675 g (1½ lb) curd ◆

METHOD

Place the butter, lemon rind, lemon juice and sugar together in an ovenproof bowl. Beat in the eggs gradually. Set the bowl over a saucepan of simmering water and cook, stirring the mixture frequently until it thickens.

Allow the curd to cool and then pour into clean, dry jars. Cover, seal and label. Store in the refrigerator.

INGREDIENTS

100 g (4 oz) unsalted butter
Grated rind and juice of 4 lemons
450 g (1 lb) sugar
4 medium eggs, lightly beaten

INGREDIENTS
450 g (1 lb) finely chopped
  suet
450 g (1 lb) currants
450 g (1 lb) raisins
450 g (1 lb) eating apples,
  peeled, cored and chopped
450 g (1 lb) caster sugar
225 g (8 oz) sultanas
100 g (4 oz) mixed candied
  peel
Grated rind and juice of 2
  lemons
150 ml ($\frac{1}{4}$ pt) brandy
5 ml (1 tsp) ground nutmeg
$\frac{1}{2}$ tsp ground cloves
$\frac{1}{2}$ tsp ground cinnamon

◆ MINCEMEAT ◆

Make this mincemeat at least 1 month before using, if possible. It is delicious used in the open mincemeat tart on page 78.

◆ **Preparation** 15–20 minutes ◆ **Makes** 2 kg (4$\frac{1}{2}$–5 lb) mincemeat ◆

METHOD
Mix all the ingredients together until well blended. Press into clean, dry, warm jars and place wax discs on top of each jar, making them as airtight as possible. Cover, seal and label.

Keep in a cool, dry place for at least 1 month before using, as the flavours need time to blend together.

INGREDIENTS
1.15 kg (2$\frac{1}{2}$ lb) dried peaches
4 ltr (7 pt) water
432 g (15.25 oz) can of
  crushed pineapple
Grated rind and juice of 2
  lemons
2.7 kg (6 lb) preserving sugar

PINEAPPLE & ◆ PEACH JAM ◆

This jam can be made at any time of the year as it uses dried peaches and canned pineapple.

◆ **Preparation and cooking** 24 hours to soak fruit, plus 1 hour ◆
◆ **Makes** 2.25–2.7 kg (5–6 lb) jam ◆

METHOD
Place the peaches in a saucepan, cover with the water and soak for about 24 hours.

Cook slowly, covered, for 20–25 minutes until tender. Drain, reserving the juice. Chop the peaches into small pieces and return to the pan with the cooking juice.

Add to the pan the pineapple, including the juice from the can, the lemon juice, rind and the sugar. Mix well together. Bring to the boil and boil hard for 20 minutes.

Leave to cool for 5–10 minutes in the pan and pour into clean, dry, warm jars. Place wax discs on top of each jar and then cover, seal and label.

◆ RASPBERRY JAM ◆

Raspberries do not contain very much pectin, but the addition of pectin-rich redcurrant juice helps to set the jam and also gives it an interesting flavour.

◆ **Preparation and cooking** 45–55 minutes ◆ **Makes** 3.6 kg (8 lb) jam ◆

METHOD

First, make the redcurrant juice. Place the redcurrants in a saucepan over a very low heat. Bring to the boil and wait until the juice flows freely from the fruit. Strain through a muslin bag or clean cloth, pressing the fruit carefully to obtain the maximum amount of juice.

Place the raspberries in a preserving pan and bring gently to the boil. Simmer for 15 minutes, stirring frequently.

Add the sugar and redcurrant juice and simmer again for 20–30 minutes. Start testing for setting point after 20 minutes. Remove the pan from the heat and spoon a little jam on to a cold plate or saucer and allow to cool. The jam is ready if a skin forms and wrinkles when pushed with a finger. Skim off any foam that appears.

When ready, pour into clean, dry, warm jars. Place wax discs on top of each jar, cover, seal and label.

INGREDIENTS

1–1.5 ltr (2 pt) redcurrants, with stalks removed
1.8 kg (4 lb) raspberries, hulled
1.8 kg (4 lb) preserving sugar

◆ STRAWBERRY JAM ◆

Choose small, firm and ripe (but not over-ripe) fruit.

◆ **Preparation and cooking** 1 hour to soak fruit, plus 15–20 minutes ◆
◆ **Makes** 4.5 kg (10 lb) jam ◆

METHOD

Place the strawberries in a preserving pan with the sugar and lemon juice. Stand for about 1 hour, stirring occasionally.

Cook over a low heat until the sugar has dissolved and then add the butter. This stops too much foam forming on top. Bring to the boil and boil hard for 4–5 minutes. Remove from the heat and add the pectin. Mix thoroughly.

Leave to cool for 30 minutes. Stir gently and then pour into clean, dry, warm jars. Place wax discs on top of each jar, cover, seal and label.

INGREDIENTS

2 kg (4½ lb) strawberries, hulled
2.7 kg (6 lb) preserving sugar
90 ml (3½ fl oz) lemon juice
25 g (1 oz) butter
1 bottle of pectin

PASTRY

Recipes are given here for all the basic pastries: shortcrust, rich shortcrust, choux, flaky, puff and rough puff. The shortcrust, flaky, puff and rough puff pastries are all suitable for both sweet and savoury dishes. All will keep for a few days in the refrigerator and freeze well, so it is worth making plenty and storing the surplus for another time.

There are a few points to remember when making pastry. The secret of good, light pastry is the amount of cold air trapped in the mixture. The cooler the ingredients, utensils and hands, the lighter the pastry will be. Handle the pastry as little as possible, and use a knife or pastry blender to cut the fat into the flour if your hands tend to be warm. Use only as much water as is necessary to bind the dough together, as too much water can make the pastry hard. If possible, always chill the pastry for at least 15 minutes before rolling out, to allow it to rest. For details on kneading, rolling out and lining tins, see pages 22–23.

INGREDIENTS
50 g (2 oz) butter
225 ml (8 fl oz) water
Good pinch of salt
100 g (4 oz) plain flour, sifted
1 medium egg yolk
2 medium eggs, beaten

◆ CHOUX PASTRY ◆

This is used for éclairs, profiteroles, choux buns, etc. It is important to add the first egg yolk while the mixture is hot enough to cook it slightly, and to beat in plenty of air after the rest of the eggs are added. An electric hand beater is best for this. Choux pastry should be baked in a hot oven, 400–425°F (200–220°C/Gas 6–7).

◆ **Preparation and cooking** 20–25 minutes, including cooling ◆
◆ **Makes** 450 g (1 lb) pastry ◆

METHOD
Place the butter, water and salt in a saucepan and bring to the boil. Remove from the heat and add all the flour at once. Beat with a wooden spoon until the mixture is smooth and leaves the sides of the pan clean.

Add the egg yolk immediately and beat thoroughly with an electric beater. Gradually add the other eggs, beating hard after each addition. Continue beating until glossy and smooth, about 1½–2 minutes. Allow the pastry to cool, about 15–20 minutes, but use while still tepid.

♦ FLAKY PASTRY ♦

This pastry is normally used for sausage rolls, sweet and savoury pies, tarts, turnovers, etc. It is usually glazed with beaten egg and baked in a hot oven, 425°F (220°C/Gas 7). The pastry will keep for 3–4 days wrapped in the refrigerator and can be frozen for several months.

♦ **Preparation** 1¾–2 hours, including chilling ♦ **Makes** 900 g (2 lb) pastry ♦

METHOD

Mix together the flour and salt. Divide the fat into 4 portions. Rub or cut 1 portion into the flour. Mix in the lemon juice and cold water and bind together to a soft dough, similar in consistency to butter. Knead lightly on a floured board until really smooth.

Roll out the dough to a rectangle 3 times longer than it is wide. Use the second portion of fat to dot the top two-thirds of the dough. Fold up the bottom third of the dough and fold down the top third. Seal the edges with the rolling pin. Wrap in a plastic bag and chill for 15 minutes in the refrigerator.

Place the dough on a floured board, with the folded edges to your left and right. Roll out into a long strip again and repeat the dotting with the third portion of fat, folding and chilling again. Repeat the whole process once more, using the remaining portion of fat. Wrap again and chill for ¾–1 hour before using.

INGREDIENTS

450 g (1 lb) plain flour, sifted, plus 50–75 g (2–3 oz) to flour board

½ tsp salt

350 g (12 oz) butter, or half butter and half lard, softened

5 ml (1 tsp) freshly squeezed lemon juice

275 ml (½ pt) cold water

♦ PUFF PASTRY ♦

This is used for vol-au-vent cases, cream slices, fruit tartlets and pies. It is a good idea to make a large quantity of puff pastry as it takes so much time and care to prepare. Spare pastry will keep well in the freezer, or in the refrigerator for a few days wrapped in foil. For the best results, make the pastry over 2 days, rolling 3 times and chilling overnight before completing the rolling the next day. Puff pastry should be cooked in a hot oven, 450°F (230°C/Gas 8).

♦ **Preparation** 4 hours, including chilling ♦ **Makes** 900 g (2 lb) pastry ♦

METHOD

Mix the flour and salt together in a bowl. Add 50 g (2 oz) of the butter, cut into small pieces, and rub or cut in until the mixture resembles fine breadcrumbs. Mix in the lemon juice and enough of the iced water to form a soft dough. The consistency should be soft, similar to that of butter. Knead lightly into a ball in the bowl.

INGREDIENTS

450 g (1 lb) plain flour, sifted, plus 50–75 g (2–3 oz) to flour board

5 ml (1 tsp) salt

450 g (1 lb) butter, softened

5 ml (1 tsp) freshly squeezed lemon juice

About 80 ml (3 fl oz) iced water

Continued overleaf

Press the remaining butter firmly in a floured cloth to remove any moisture and shape it into a rectangle.

Roll out the dough on a floured board to a rectangle, slightly wider than the butter and about twice its length. Place the butter on one half of the pastry, fold the other half over and press the edges together with the rolling pin. Leave in a cool place for 15–20 minutes to allow the butter to harden slightly.

Roll out the pastry to a long strip, 3 times its original length, but keeping the width the same. It is important to keep the corners square and the sides straight so that the pastry is of an even thickness; the butter must not break through the dough. Fold the bottom third up and the top third down, press the edges together with the rolling pin and chill for 30 minutes inside a well oiled plastic bag.

Place the dough on a floured board with the folded edges to your left and right. Roll out into a long strip and fold again into 3, as above. Chill for a further 30 minutes. Repeat this process 4 more times and chill for a final 30 minutes before using.

◆ RICH SHORTCRUST PASTRY ◆

This is perfect for sweet flans and tarts where a richer, softer pastry than shortcrust is required. It is a good idea to work on a flat board rather than in a bowl when mixing the dough. Rich shortcrust pastry is usually baked in a moderately hot oven, 400°F (200°C/Gas 6).
To bake blind (or unfilled), place a circle of greaseproof paper over the pastry and cover with a layer of dried or baking beans. Bake at 400°F (200°C/Gas 6) for 15–20 minutes. Remove the beans and paper, reduce the oven to 350°F (180°C/Gas 4) and bake for a further 10–15 minutes for the base to dry out.

◆ **Preparation** 25 minutes, including chilling ◆ **Makes** 450 g (1 lb) pastry ◆

INGREDIENTS
225 g (8 oz) plain flour, sifted
Good pinch of salt
175 g (6 oz) butter, softened
1 medium egg yolk
10 ml (2 tsp) caster sugar
About 15–30 ml (1–2 tbsp)
    cold water

METHOD
Mix together the flour and salt. Rub or cut in the butter until the mixture resembles fine breadcrumbs. Make a well in the middle and put in the egg yolk. Sprinkle the caster sugar over. With a knife, gradually mix into the flour.

Mix in enough water, a little at a time, to form a stiff but pliable dough. Knead lightly, wrap in foil and chill in the refrigerator for at least 15 minutes.

◆ ROUGH PUFF PASTRY ◆

This is quicker and easier to make than puff pastry but gives less rise. It is ideal for pies and tarts and is used as an alternative to shortcrust pastry for such things as mince pies or sausage rolls. The pastry is usually baked in a very hot oven, 450°F (230°C/Gas 8).

◆ **Preparation** 1½–1¾ hours, including chilling ◆ **Makes** 450 g (1 lb) pastry ◆

INGREDIENTS
225 g (8 oz) plain flour, sifted, plus 50–75 g (2–3 oz) to flour board
Pinch of salt
175 g (6 oz) butter, or half butter and half lard, softened
½ tsp freshly squeezed lemon juice
About 30–45 ml (2–3 tbsp) cold water

METHOD
Mix together the flour and salt. Cut the fat into walnut-sized pieces. and stir lightly into the flour with a round-bladed knife. Make a well in the middle. Mix in the lemon juice and enough cold water to form an elastic dough.

Roll the dough out on a floured board to a long strip, keeping the corners as square as possible and the sides straight. Fold the bottom third up and the top third down and turn the dough so that the folded edges are on your left and right.

Repeat this rolling and folding process 3 more times, if possible, leaving 15 minutes between the second and third and between the third and fourth rolling. Chill for at least 15 minutes before using.

◆ SHORTCRUST PASTRY ◆

Shortcrust pastry is used for savoury and sweet flans, tarts, pies and sausage rolls. It can be made with all margarine or all butter, or with a mixture of lard and margarine or butter, as here. For savoury pies, tarts and flans, a little spice or chopped herbs can be added to the mixture.
Shortcrust pastry is usually baked in a hot oven, 425–450°F (220–230°C/Gas 7–8) for the first 15–20 minutes, until set; then in a slightly cooler oven, 400°F (200°C/Gas 6) for the required time.
Bake blind as for rich shortcrust pastry, opposite.

◆ **Preparation** 20 minutes, including chilling ◆ **Makes** 350 g (12 oz) pastry ◆

INGREDIENTS
225 g (8 oz) plain flour, sifted
Pinch of salt
50 g (2 oz) margarine or butter, softened
50 g (2 oz) lard, softened
About 30 ml (2 tbsp) cold water

METHOD
Mix the flour and salt together in a bowl. Cut the fats into small pieces and rub or cut into the flour until the mixture resembles breadcrumbs. Gradually add enough water, mixing with a fork, to form a stiff but pliable dough.

Knead lightly for a few minutes until smooth, but do not over-knead as this can make the pastry tough. Wrap in foil and refrigerate for at least 15 minutes.

INDEX

◆ ACKNOWLEDGEMENTS ◆

Author's acknowledgements
I would like to thank both Sam Twining and The Tea Council
for information about tea; Lucinda Elborne and Joan
Mulrooney for help with cake preparation and trying out ideas;
Stephen Harvey for the loan of 1930s china, and Keith Cavers
for help with research and the loan of historical material. I
would also like to thank Pam Norris for instigating the book
and for her help and support during the writing; David Holmes
and Clifford Lee, my partners at Tea-Time, for their support
during the writing and for all the fun we have at Tea-Time, and
finally the staff for contributing to the success of Tea-Time and
for their hard work while I was busy writing and testing
the recipes.

Dorling Kindersley would like to thank:
Pamela Norris, for her work in initiating the book, Royal
Worcester Spode and Chinacraft, 130 New Bond Street, London W1, for loan of china for photographs, TWININGS, with
special thanks to Sam Twining for his help and assistance.

Photography: James Murphy
Food preparation for photography: Nigel Slater
Stylist: Andrea Lampton, Sarah Wiley
Illustrations: Antonia Enthoven

Typesetting: Advanced Filmsetters (Glasgow) Ltd
Reproduction: Repro Llovet, Barcelona